P9-EJS-474

Contents

Dedication

To my sisters, Bernadette Larivière and Margaret Kelly-Smith; our shared youth is a precious history

Acknowledgements

TO MY FAMILY, WHO HAD TO RELY ON PHOTOS TO CONJURE UP my image during my long writing absences in the upper reaches of the house;

To Faye Boer of Folklore Publishing, for letting me work my way through this manuscript with maximum support and minimal interruption;

To my gracious and ever-vigilant editor Audrey McClellan, who does what she does so well;

To the kind librarians at Pembina Trail Public Library in Winnipeg, for their patience with my demands and their forgiveness for my occasional lapses in character;

And finally, to all the Great Canadians whose stories have not appeared in this book.

Introduction

WHEN COMPILING ANY LIST OF "GREATS," THE QUESTION OF criteria is sure to emerge. The CBC's Canada-wide "The Greatest Canadian" competition in 2004, was actually of little help. Although those making nominations were required to state reasons for their choices, there were no specific guidelines for inclusion. The exercise, fun as it was, was little more than a popularity contest, and those who made the list got there for reasons that were, in some cases, thinly disguised attempts to poke fun at the entire process.

So my research began with the question: What constitutes a Great Canadian? A short list of criteria emerged, based on the idea that, to be considered great, the individuals must have contributed something significant to Canadian society—something that has an impact on us today in our daily lives. I decided that individuals selected for this volume must

a) have a name that is widely recognized in Canada, and

b) have contributed in a significant and positive way to Canadian culture or life.

And the search began. The CBC Top Ten list was a start. It provided a solid number of our country's leaders and decision-makers from all parts of the political spectrum. I added a number of activists and, to round out the group, a writer, a philosopher and an athlete. Voilà! A cross-section of Canadian greats.

The list ended there, but the questions didn't. As I pored over the sourcebooks, more and more questions plagued me: What exactly is greatness? Is it a matter of intellect? Or personality? Is it that nebulous thing called charisma? What determines greatness? Does greatness run in families? Are so-called great people born with an insatiable desire to do something memorable? Is it environment that brings out greatness? Does happenstance create situations into which ambitious people can insert themselves and shine? Do those we call "great" have singular focus and an inordinate amount of drive? Could it be that greatness evolves from one of these situations, or two of them? Or could it be that greatness is a happy, coincidental convergence of all of them?

To probe further for an answer to these questions, I reviewed the lives of the individuals I had researched and written about to see if they shared any characteristics. On the surface there appeared to be little in common between the poor Métis boy and the son of a multi-millionaire, or between people whose education consisted of less than five years of schooling and those with several degrees; between people with lonely personal lives and those with rich and rewarding family lives; between those who made their impact while very young and those who did not reach their stride until after middle age. They seemed at first glance a disparate bunch.

But on closer examination, I began to see some common threads:

- All of them had a belief system of some kind that enabled them to see themselves as part of something much larger and more significant.

- They all had tremendous energy.

- They all had support, whether from family or friends or followers. They had at least one arm to lean on, one shoulder to cry on and one hand to hold.

- They all had healthy egos. Without sufficient sense of self, perhaps the greatest Canadians would not have been so great at all.

- All dealt with controversy, whether it was in the form of physical aggression, intellectual disagreement or a struggle for rights.

There was one more aspect to the lives of these great people that seemed to bind them together—the timeliness of their actions. Each of these Great Canadians came along at a time when Canada truly needed them, whether to speak for rights or to prevent a world war; whether to open our eyes to the potential destruction of our planet or open our wallets to cure a rampaging disease; whether to fight for justice or to invigorate patriotism.

Canada will always need people to defend the rights, freedoms and resources our ancestors fought so hard to preserve, and that, perhaps, is the most uplifting aspect of compiling a book such as this. There will always be someone out there who is doing great things for this country. And for that reason, a book like this will never be finished.

As I compiled the list, it became clear that gender balance was going to be a problem. Again, the CBC list was of little assistance as there was not one woman named in its Top Ten. This lack of women surprised me, particularly as I wrote the Nellie McClung chapter that celebrated how far women have come since the beginning of the 20th century. Why, in 2005, was it so difficult to find women to include in a list of Great Canadians?

To give myself some focus on the issue, I decided to put the question to a number of friends and colleagues, both male and female. The responses were thought-provoking:

- The criteria themselves are male-oriented, effectively eliminating most women from consideration.

- Even though women are working outside the home, they retain primary responsibility for their homes and families. They are too busy taking care of those close to them to get involved in causes.

- Women's strength is not measured in how they deal with issues, but rather in how they deal with people. Success is measured in terms of issues.

- Women have had unequal opportunities to excel and they have simply not yet caught up with men.

- Women are still often chastised for spending any effort or time outside their homes.

- Men are reluctant to listen to women's ideas, so their ideas often do not reach fruition. If the ideas do reach fruition, someone else will be there to take the credit while the woman is off doing something else.

- Timing has often been right for men to step in and take credit for pulling together projects for which others (including women) have done the groundwork.

- Women are still brought up to nurture. They often work quietly, behind the scenes, leaving the glory and publicity for others.

- Women tend to work best in groups, so are rarely singled out for individual praise.

Whatever the reasons, women were in short supply for inclusion on this Great Canadian list. If you would like to suggest names for a future book on Great Women of Canada, please forward your ideas by e-mail, giving a brief explanation for your choice, to Faye Boer at Folklore Publishing (fboer@folklorepublishing.com).

CHAPTER ONE

Margaret Atwood
(1939–)

I am a writer, and a reader, and that's about it.

–Margaret Atwood

BORN ON NOVEMBER 18, 1939, IN OTTAWA, ONTARIO, Margaret Eleanor Atwood claims that her childhood, filled as it was with books and solitude, was a perfect training ground for a writer. Her father, Carl Edward Atwood, an entomologist, ran a forest insect research station in northern Ontario. For several months of every year during the first few years of Margaret's life, the Atwoods and their two small children trundled off to the wilderness.

In 1946, when Margaret was just seven years old and her brother, Harold, was nine, their father took a position on the faculty of the University of Toronto, and the family moved to the city. Until her younger sister, Ruth, came along in 1951, Margaret's closest companions were her mother and her brother. Both, in their own ways, encouraged her interest in reading and writing. Her mother, Margaret Dorothy, celebrated quietness in children, so Margaret was rarely chided for reading. Harold often entertained his sister on silent summer evenings in the woods by telling her stories.

Margaret's first forays into writing came early. When she was seven, she wrote a play and performed it with puppets she'd made. The performance was not received with exceptional critical acclaim by the small audience consisting of her brother and his friends, but the experience fuelled Margaret's desire to write more.

Margaret's secondary school years were spent at Leaside High School in Toronto, where she was active in basketball, choir and various clubs. Her writing at this time was fairly eclectic and included what Atwood herself described as borderline literary material, written under pseudonyms.

For no memorable reason, Atwood, a home economics major, had a sudden shift in awareness in 1955. As she told interviewer Linda Sandler in 1977: "It was about that time I realized I didn't want to be a home economist; I wanted to be a writer."

In 1957 Margaret enrolled in Victoria College, University of Toronto, where she discovered Canadian literature. Rubbing shoulders with such notable Canadian writers as Northrop Frye, Jay Macpherson, Kathleen Coburn and Dennis Lee enhanced her appreciation of her studies. In 1961 her suite of poems entitled *Double Persephone* was published and won the E.J. Pratt Medal from the University of Toronto. She had a number of other poems published around the same time in various distinguished literary journals, including *Canadian Forum* and *Tamarack Review.*

With her honours BA in English completed, she left Toronto in 1961 to pursue an MA in Victorian literature at Radcliffe College (Harvard) under a one-year Woodrow Wilson Fellowship. Upon completing her master's degree, she worked for some time in Toronto, and in 1964 spent a year at the University of British Columbia, lecturing in the English department. It was at UBC that she began the initial draft of *The Edible Woman.* She returned to Harvard in 1965 to continue studies toward her PhD.

In the next two years, her literary life blossomed. *The Circle Game*, her first major collection of poetry, was published in 1966 to critical acclaim. The following year she received the Governor General's Award for Poetry and Chicago's Union Poetry Prize for *The Circle Game* and first prize in the Centennial Commission Poetry Competition for *The Animals in That Country,* another poetry collection. She left Harvard in 1967 and began to teach, first at Sir George Williams University in Montréal, where she taught literature, and then at the University of Alberta in Edmonton, where she taught creative writing.

In 1967 Atwood married James Polk, an American writer she met at Harvard. They were divorced in 1973. During those years her literary life soared.

The Edible Woman was finally published in 1969 by McClelland and Stewart. That first published novel provided Atwood with an unexpected opportunity. She sold film rights to the book for $15,000, which gave her, at age 30, the freedom to spend several months in Europe, travelling to England, France and Italy, gathering experiences that later fuelled her writing of *Lady Oracle*.

On her return to Canada in 1970, Atwood resumed teaching literature and creative writing as writer-in-residence at York University in Toronto and, the following year, at the University of Toronto. At the same time she served as an editor and member of the board of directors for House of Anansi Press.

Over the next few years, Atwood was prolific. By the time she was 35 years old she had garnered several literary prizes, written a televised play and published eight collections of poetry and three novels in addition to numerous short stories and essays. She continued to teach and study, and in 1976, she gave birth to Jess, her daughter with partner, novelist Graeme Gibson. Motherhood temporarily changed her focus. For nearly two years, her public appearances dropped off. Her explanation to Linda Sandler at the time was typical of the caustic comments Margaret Atwood appeared to be fond of making: "I feel I made my statement, did my thing...and I'm quite happy to sit back now and watch other people attacking each other."

But her hiatus didn't last long. Novels published during the 1980s included Atwood's political thriller *Bodily Harm* (1981) and *Cat's Eye* in 1988, which received the 1989 City of Toronto Book Award. A children's book, *Anna's Pet*, was published in 1980. The short-story collection *Dancing Girls* appeared in 1983, and *True Stories*, a book of poetry, in 1981. The highly acclaimed speculative fiction novel *The Handmaid's Tale* (1985) was performed as a play in London, England, and later made into a Hollywood movie and an opera. It was shortlisted for the Booker Prize and awarded the 1986 Governor General's Award.

The 1990s were no less prolific. Two short-story collections, *Wilderness Tips* (1991) and *Bluebeard's Egg* (1993), were followed by two novels, *The Robber Bride* (1993) and *Alias Grace* (1996), which won the Giller Prize. Her children's books during this decade included *For the Birds* (1990) and *Princess Prunella and the Purple Peanut* (1995). In the 1990s Atwood was the recipient of the Order of Ontario, the Molson Award and the Chevalier dans l'Ordre des Arts et des Lettres. Shortlisted three previous times for the Booker Prize, Atwood finally won the honour in 2000 for her novel *The Blind Assassin*, which also won the Dashiell Hammett Award.

The CBC Archives website refers to Margaret Atwood, poet, novelist, critic, as the "Queen of Can Lit." She continues to entertain as she challenges her readers to consider issues important to all humanity. In recent years she has given generously of her time and energy to causes such as Amnesty International and the Canadian Civil Liberties Association. Also involved with organizations specifically focused on issues of concern to writers, she served as president of PEN International from 1984 to 1986, and chair of the Writers Union of Canada from 1981 to 1982.

With her books now translated into more than 35 languages, Margaret Atwood continues to provide the literary world with a significant volume of work that expresses what she holds dear: peace, freedom, social justice and quiet revolution. And she continues to speak to her readers as individuals. As she wrote in *Negotiating With the Dead:*

> *The ideal reader may prove to be anyone at all—any one at all—because the art of reading is just as singular—always—as the act of writing.*

CHAPTER TWO

Tommy Douglas
(1904–1986)

"Watch out for the little fellow with an idea."

–Tommy Douglas

CANADIANS WHO TAKE PRIDE IN OUR UNIVERSAL HEALTH-CARE system must thank a diminutive prairie man who had big ideas. Born on October 20, 1904, Thomas Clement Douglas was just seven years old when he immigrated to Canada with his family from his birthplace, Falkirk, Scotland, settling in Winnipeg in 1911.

At the age of 10, Tommy was diagnosed with osteomyelitis, a chronic bone infection in his leg that required several operations. Unable to afford the expensive and ongoing surgery, Tommy's family had to face the possibility that their son would have his leg amputated. Luckily, a visiting doctor who knew of their plight offered to perform for free an experimental surgery that saved Tommy's leg. This experience may have contributed to Tommy's later conviction that all Canadians should have whatever hospital care they needed, regardless of their ability to pay.

The Douglas family went back to Scotland in 1914 for the duration of World War I, returning to Winnipeg in 1919 in time to witness the Winnipeg General Strike, in which workers marched in the streets to protest conditions in the factories. The strike culminated on June 21, a day now remembered as Bloody Saturday, when 35,000 protesting workers confronted the Royal North-West Mounted Police in Winnipeg's downtown. In the ensuing battle, one man was killed and 29 were injured.

Frightening as it was, the event fostered in Tommy Douglas a lifelong interest in the plight of the common man. The small, sensitive teenager, 14 at the time, was delivering newspapers when the riot broke out. He and a friend climbed to the roof of a downtown building to watch. From their ringside seat, they saw the workers gain strength and momentum after hearing rousing speeches from people like J.S. Woodsworth, a Methodist minister who had a gift for oration. Listening to Woodsworth challenge the established order with a series of passionate yet valid arguments, Tommy received his first vivid lesson in the power of personal conviction.

But it wasn't yet time for Tommy Douglas to enter the political arena. He was much too busy. In 1919 he began work as a printer's apprentice at Richardson Press in Winnipeg. His father had just returned from the war and was making meagre pay as an ironworker. Tommy was his family's major breadwinner, handing over most of his

salary to his mother to help pay the bills and see
to the education of his two sisters. He took classes
in the evenings to learn the printing business, was
an active member of the Baptist Church, attended
meetings of the Order of DeMolay (the youth wing
of the Masonic Lodge), took lessons in elocution,
studied the clarinet and was a Boy Scout leader in
a local troop. He read voraciously and even tried
his hand at acting. In addition to all his other activities, Tommy trained and competed in the sport of
boxing, a pursuit that won him the Manitoba ama-
teur flyweight title in 1922.

Two years later, with a fervour that came more
from a desire for social improvement than a religious vocation, Tommy travelled 200 kilometres
west to Brandon, Manitoba. There he enrolled in
Brandon College, a Baptist school that was affiliated
with McMaster University in Hamilton, Ontario.
Because he had never finished high school, Tommy
spent the first three years at Brandon earning his
high school certificate. In 1927, at the age of 22,
he entered the arts faculty at the same institution.

It was during the next three years that Tommy
Douglas' leadership ability made itself evident. He
was a scholar and a debater, an actor and a student
leader, and was active in the Student Christian
Movement. But his most role-defining activity during those years was his work as a supply minister
for local churches. When young Tommy Douglas
took his place in the pulpit, it was clear that his
greatest strength lay in his ability to move people

with his words. Standing room only was often the norm in the church, with many visitors in attendance from other congregations.

Upon graduation in 1930, Tommy married Irma Dempsey, a young woman he had met in Brandon where Irma was studying piano. The best man at their wedding was Stanley Knowles, a classmate and friend of Tommy's, who remained close all their lives and who later shared the stage with Tommy as one of Canada's leading socialist politicians.

Shortly after his wedding, Douglas was hired as the new preacher for Calvary Baptist Church in Weyburn, Saskatchewan. Tommy was 25 and Irma just 19 when they began their life as a married couple in the once-prosperous town that was beginning to suffer from the Great Depression. As wheat was a mainstay of the prairie economy, it wasn't long before the fall of grain prices took its toll on the community. When severe drought hit, followed by grasshopper plagues and catastrophic windstorms, the prairies were in deep trouble.

While the dustbowl farmers around him were struggling to make enough money to buy food staples, Tommy Douglas was earning a fairly good salary of $1800 a year, which was supplemented by the fees Irma earned as a piano teacher. However, their comfort did not blind them to the plight of their neighbours. They were generous with their time and money and pitched in with energy, cheerfulness and optimism to help their community in any way they could.

As the hard times continued and desperate prairie farmers felt as though their God had forsaken them, church attendance began to decline. Out of a heartfelt need to help his parishioners, Tommy's sermons contained less and less dogma and began to feature practical solutions.

While continuing his studies by correspondence for a master's degree from McMaster University, he immersed himself in local action against poverty. He collaborated with citizens from various walks of life who were determined to change the social order. He collected clothing and food for the poor, lobbied local authorities and did his best to inform every person he came into contact with of the need for change to the economic system that had brought the prairies to its knees.

In September 1931, Tommy Douglas witnessed another strike that convinced him of the need for more immediate action. Shortly after returning from Chicago, where he went to register in a PhD program in sociology, Douglas was made aware of the plight of workers in the coalfields around Estevan, Saskatchewan. As in the 1919 Winnipeg strike, workers sought relief from the inhumane working conditions that had arisen in the dustbowl. Employers knew men were desperate for work. If one man didn't like the conditions, there were 10 others who would happily take his place. Workers were treated like slaves or chattels. Forced to give over large portions of their already meagre hourly pay for doctor's fees, tools and machinery, many men went home almost empty-handed at the end of a gruelling workweek. When the workers had had enough, they marched in protest, only to be beaten back by police, leaving 23 of their number injured and three dead.

Tommy Douglas knew something had to be done. One of the causes that concerned him most was medical care. People who were badly in need of medical help did not go to hospital because most, like his own family, could not afford the costs. Hospitals, in turn, could not afford to offer free treatment. They had to pay staff and provide food, bedding and equipment. Rallying people he knew, Douglas was able to gather donations of food, money and volunteer time, but it was not enough.

He turned for help to M.J. Coldwell, a school principal from Regina, who was a leader in the Saskatchewan Teachers' Federation and president of the Independent Labour Party. Together, Douglas and Coldwell organized the Weyburn Independent Labour Party, which maintained close and mutually supportive contact with Coldwell's group in Regina. By 1932 they had reorganized and regrouped several times, finally joining forces with Labour Party delegates from Alberta, Manitoba and British Columbia to form the Co-operative Commonwealth Federation (CCF), which had its first annual general meeting in Regina in July 1933.

The creation of this new party might have been the beginning of a political career for T.C. Douglas, but he was still too busy with other concerns. In addition to his congregational work, Tommy was working hard to complete his degree in sociology, and Tommy and Irma were preparing for the birth of their first child.

The Douglases' daughter Shirley was born in April 1934,* and in June Tommy's CCF friends convinced him to run for the party in the upcoming provincial election. He campaigned hard but lost the election. One of Tommy's biographers, Dave Margoshes, reported that Douglas later summed up his failure on the campaign trail: "[I was] like a university professor giving a course in sociology....I'm sure half the people didn't know what I was talking about."

With a bad taste in his mouth from the provincial election, Tommy was not interested in pursuing a career in politics, although he agreed to take on the presidency of the youth wing of the CCF. He contemplated several career options: going back to school in Chicago to complete his PhD or taking a post with a church in Edmonton or a church in Milwaukee, Wisconsin. Fate stepped in to help. This time it was in the form of a Baptist

---

* Shirley Douglas pursued an acting career, becoming a well-known name in Canadian stage and film productions. She married and later divorced Donald Sutherland, a Canadian actor who achieved international stardom. Shirley has three children: Tom (Tad), Joan and movie and television actor Kiefer Sutherland.

church superintendent who came to talk Tommy out of politics. He threatened that if Douglas ever again ran for a party that supported what the superintendent referred to as communist-inspired political thinking, Douglas would never preach another sermon in Canada. The superintendent had misjudged the diminutive man's spirit. A few days later, Douglas signed up to be Weyburn's CCF candidate in the 1935 federal election.

It was not a smooth run. Realizing early on that the Liberals were well positioned to win, Douglas promised to support Social Credit legislation in exchange for that party's support of his candidacy. His CCF colleagues were furious, and the move almost resulted in his ejection from the CCF. Instead, it won him the election and a seat in Parliament. Tommy Douglas was off to Ottawa.

He gave his first parliamentary speech on February 6, 1936, and soon after began making a nuisance of himself, according to the Liberals. He was vocal and quick, and along with the four other CCF members who were elected to Parliament, he pressed the government to give a good account of itself. The small group could do little to change votes in Parliament, but it did its best to encourage those making decisions to consider their options more carefully.

In autumn 1939, Canada was plunged into World War II, and local concerns were temporarily set aside as the great majority of eligible men and many women enlisted. Tommy Douglas signed up with the South Saskatchewan Regiment and quickly rose to the rank of captain. But he never saw active duty. Shortly before he was to ship out with the Winnipeg Grenadiers, his tour was cancelled because of the old weakness in his right knee. He spent the remainder of his military service training troops and the following year was thrust into an election that had been hastily called by Mackenzie King's Liberals.

Douglas was elected by a margin of 950 votes, returning to a Parliament that was richer by three CCF members. But even with the increase in numbers, the CCF knew it would have to fight hard to have any influence over the federal Liberals, who had achieved the largest majority of any Canadian government to that time. The CCF didn't manage to change much policy, but it got Canadians, particularly Western Canadians, thinking about issues that affected them.

By 1944, William Patterson, Saskatchewan's Liberal premier, had overstayed his welcome. With an election platform that promised what amounted to a western utopia, 39-year-old Tommy Douglas was poised to be the West's redeemer. That summer he became Canada's first socialist premier in a provincial election that many said was long overdue. In spring 1945, Douglas became the father of another daughter, Joan.* That same year, his party

* Joan Douglas Tulchinsky trained as a nurse. She moved to Israel with her husband and their two sons.

introduced major reforms that fulfilled or took steps to deliver on its campaign promises.

By the end of its first year in power, the government had issued cards that gave 30,000 people access to free medical services. It had increased the mother's allowance by 20 percent and set up a province-wide insurance corporation, which later set the stage for the establishment of Crown corporations. Roads were paved; electricity and sewer services were provided; and the provincial debt was greatly reduced. The Saskatchewan cabinet was increased to include new departments of labour and social welfare, and Douglas did not hesitate to appoint non-CCF members as experts in various departments. To pay for the changes, Douglas decreased ministerial salaries, including his own. Everywhere Premier Douglas went, people rallied to cheer him and his government.

Saskatchewan continued to prosper under his leadership. Re-elected for a total of four terms, Douglas led his province through 17 successful years of socialist government.

But there was still work to do. By the late 1950s, Douglas was pushing hard for Saskatchewan to adopt a total medical care system, while at the same time urging the federal government to follow suit. Some of his strongest opponents were fellow Saskatchewanites, who feared the financial stresses the program would place on the already

burdened provincial budget. That group included
most of the province's doctors, who waged a major
campaign against the CCF in the June 1960 election, featuring state health insurance as the major
issue. The Saskatchewan College of Physicians and
Surgeons warned voters that a CCF win would
lead to a massive out-migration of physicians, with
hospital spots being taken by less-experienced
immigrant doctors. Their tactics failed to dissuade
staunch CCF supporters, and Douglas and his party
were re-elected.

On November 1, 1961, Douglas resigned as premier after winning the leadership of the New
Democratic Party, a newly constituted party unit-
ing the CCF with labour unions. Days later, the
medicare bill was passed by Saskatchewan's parliament. In July 1962, after a brief time during
which the province's doctors went on strike to
protest it, the Medical Care Insurance Act came
into force on the foundation built by Tommy
Douglas. Saskatchewan had finally won what
Douglas had been fighting for more than 30 years to
achieve, but he himself had lost. Running as the
NDP candidate for Regina in the June 1962 federal
election called by Conservative prime minister John
Diefenbaker, Tommy Douglas was beaten. He didn't
stay down for long.

The NDP held its first national convention in
Ottawa two months later. It was the first bilingual
event of its kind ever held in the country, hosting
more than 2000 delegates from across Canada and

featuring marching bands, banners and catchy campaign slogans. But it wasn't enough. In a country with an economy that was booming with post-war riches and where unemployment was at an all-time low, people had become complacent. Left-wing tactics were seen as radical, an unnecessary disturbance to the peace and harmony of adequate government. The mood had changed. Douglas was no longer seen as a saviour. Although still popular as a speaker and well liked as a man, Tommy Douglas no longer had the unwavering support of the masses. His once shiny sword had lost its sheen.

Realizing his leader would not be elected if left to the prairie voters, Erhart Regier, a loyal Douglas supporter from British Columbia, resigned his federal seat in Burnaby-Coquitlam. In the resulting by-election, Douglas won the seat by a wide margin and was returned to Parliament, where he resumed his fight for change. The change for which he is most remembered and revered was the Canada-wide Medical Care Act established in 1966.

His last decade in Ottawa was not marked by the great changes he had seen in the early years of his political life, but Tommy Douglas remained a vocal and honest opponent of capitalism. He managed, at the age of 63, to win some points against the fiery young Pierre Elliott Trudeau in a heated tele-vised debate in 1968. The Liberals under Trudeau won support in the rest of Canada, but Douglas' legacy of NDP strength prevailed on the prairies.

Douglas went on to two more election victories and took his final position as NDP energy critic in 1969, remaining in the post until 1979, when he retired from politics. Over the years, Douglas earned numerous honours and awards for his work to improve the lives of Canadians. He was made a Companion of the Order of Canada in 1980, was awarded a number of honorary university degrees and in 1985 received the Saskatchewan Award of Merit. Tommy Douglas died of cancer on February 24, 1986. In November 2004, in CBC's widely publicized contest of public opinion, T.C. Douglas was named "The Greatest Canadian."

Charles Lynch, columnist for the *Ottawa Citizen*, wrote after the death of this courageous politician:

As much as any man, it was Douglas who turned Canada into the most highly socialized country in the Western world, without anybody really noticing what was happening.

CHAPTER THREE

Terry Fox
(1958–1981)

I believe in miracles. I have to.

–Terry Fox

A BRIEF YET INTENSE 143 DAYS IN 1980 STAND OUT IN THE minds of Canadians. This was when a bright, handsome young man from British Columbia jog-hopped his way into newspaper headlines and into our hearts.

Terrance Stanley Fox, known as Terry, was the second of Rolly and Betty Fox's four children. Born in Winnipeg, Manitoba, on July 28, 1958, the energetic and determined youngster's parents claim they weren't surprised when he accomplished a feat that is commemorated each year around the world.

An eager and athletic human kinesiology student in his first year at Vancouver's Simon Fraser University, Terry was just 18 when doctors discovered that he had developed osteogenic sarcoma. Three weeks later, they amputated his right leg in an attempt to stop the spread of the rare cancer. The surgery was followed by weeks of intense chemotherapy, during which Terry rallied all the courage he had to fight the pain and the devastation of losing a leg. But he didn't spend all that time worrying about himself. His thoughts turned repeatedly to others he had met while in hospital—small children who were dying and older people who were in constant pain.

Within weeks of his surgery, Terry again became active in sports, participating in wheelchair games and fitness activities. As the surgery site healed and he became accustomed to the discomfort of his prosthetic leg, Terry began running. People who knew him well were not surprised when he announced that he was going to run across Canada to raise money for cancer research. Terry had always been persistent, even stubborn. If Terry Fox had convinced himself he was going to run across Canada on one leg, no one would be able to talk him out of it.

His training began in February 1979, with Terry struggling to find a comfortable way to run on an artificial leg that was not designed for such high-impact activity. The constant jolting and rubbing of the cup on the prosthesis caused his leg stump to blister and bleed. But Terry persisted until, on August 30, 1979, he finished the full course of the Prince George (BC) Marathon. In the months following the marathon, Terry got busy with his plans.

He and Doug Alward, a promising athlete and Terry's best friend since high school, contacted the local office of the Canadian Cancer Society and received the go-ahead for the run, with the proviso that they would have to raise their own funds for the trip. With their winning combination of sincerity and positive outlook, they managed to garner sponsorships from several large corporations, including a van from the Ford Motor Company, money for gas from Imperial Oil and running shoes from Adidas.

On April 12, 1980, with Doug driving the donated van, making meals and providing emotional support, Terry set out from St. John's, Newfoundland, on his cross-country odyssey, the Marathon of Hope. Although he had done what he considered plenty of planning, Terry was disappointed with the reception he got for the first few days of the run. But he took heart in Port-aux-Basques, Newfoundland, where the town's 10,000 residents handed over $10,000. It was there that Terry's goal of one dollar for every Canadian took shape.

At the end of May, Darrell, Terry's younger brother, joined the group. When they reached Montréal, the weeks of on-and-off discouragement finally ended. The president of the Four Seasons Hotel chain, Isadore Sharp, had lost his own teenage son to cancer and understood and supported what Terry was trying to do. He provided free accommodations for the three young men and spread the word about their goal of raising funds for cancer research. Then the Canadian Cancer Society contacted Terry at the hotel and asked him

to postpone his arrival in Ontario by a few days—
they had big plans.

As Terry approached Hawkesbury, Ontario, on
the last Saturday in June 1980, he knew the weeks
of pain were worth it. A brass band met the van,
and thousands of local residents lined the balloon-
festooned streets. The momentum grew as word of
the run quickly spread throughout Ontario. The
provincial police provided an escort for the duration of the run in Ontario. In Ottawa, Terry met
with Governor General Ed Schreyer and Prime
Minister Pierre Elliott Trudeau. He was the guest of
honour at several football, hockey and baseball
games, where he garnered even more support for
his cause. Donations poured in from all over the
country.

When Terry arrived in Toronto, people lined the
streets in an amazing show of support and encouragement that continued until August 31, at Thunder Bay, where Terry and his Marathon of Hope
received a crushing blow. As Terry pushed himself
to run the last few kilometres of the day, a bout of
severe coughing resulted in a quick visit to the
Thunder Bay hospital. Doctors confirmed the
worst—the cancer had spread to Terry's lungs. He
knew that after 5376 kilometres, his running was
over. What he didn't know was that thousands of
others had taken up his campaign.

As he lay in his hospital bed, going through
another round of devastating chemotherapy, he

watched celebrities such as Anne Murray, Glen Campbell, Elton John, Karen Kain and the Stratford Festival Opera Chorus perform in support of his cause. In one evening a telethon raised over $10 million dollars for cancer research. In a resounding and miraculous reaction to the televised plea, more than $25 million dollars were pledged or donated by corporations, governments and individuals.

During the remainder of the year, Terry Fox received many honours for his contribution to Canadian society. He became a Companion of the Order of Canada, was made a member of the Order of the Dogwood, British Columbia's highest honour, and was awarded the Lou Marsh Trophy for outstanding athletic achievement by the Canadian Sports Editors' Association. By February 1981, when Canada's population stood at 24.1 million, the Marathon of Hope had raised $24.7 million dollars, exceeding Terry's goal of one dollar for every Canadian. Terry Fox died on June 28, 1981, knowing that his run had been worth it.

Every year on the second Sunday after Labour Day, thousands of people in 60 countries around the world run to raise money for cancer research in recognition of the wonderful example set by Terry Fox. His legacy lives on.

CHAPTER FOUR

Wayne Gretzky
(1961–)

Of the shots you don't take, one hundred percent don't go in.

–Wayne Gretzky

NO COMPENDIUM OF GREAT CANADIANS WOULD BE COMPLETE without a chapter on the Great One himself. Walter and Phyllis Gretzky's firstborn child, the oldest of five children, skated from their little backyard rink in Brantford, Ontario, to become what many believe to be the greatest hockey player of all time.

Walter Gretzky came home from his job with the telephone company in the cold, dark dreariness of an Ontario winter. But what greeted his eyes made him as cheerful as if the sun had been shining and the temperature a balmy 20°C. There, on the backyard rink he'd made the weekend before, was five-year-old Wayne, all decked out in his bulky jersey and thick gloves, skating happily under the lights strung on a clothesline.

Walter edged closer, not wanting to disturb the concentration evident on his little boy's face. He watched proudly as Wayne shot the puck against a board propped up in one corner, and then skated into position to catch the puck when it ricocheted off. Two, three, four times—the puck hit, then careened away. Wayne always seemed to know just where it was going to end up, and he got there before it did. Walter smiled to himself. His boy was going to be famous some day; he was sure of it.

The following year, with Dad as his coach and the backyard rink as his favourite place to spend time, six-year-old Wayne Gretzky was good enough to play in the Brantford atom league on a team that was made up of mostly 10- and 11-year-old boys who were not only older, but a lot bigger. Wayne had to learn early in his career how to make up for his smaller size. He played other sports off-season and quickly discovered how to play an intellectual rather than a physical game of hockey. By the time he was 10, little Wayne had amazed everyone with 378 goals and 120 assists in 85 games. His strategy was paying off.

He also had to learn how to handle rivalry that came not just from the opposing side, but also from his own teammates and their parents, who resented his ability to capture the spotlight at every game. He learned that jealousy was part of the game, and if he wanted to be number one, there would be resentful people. He decided to ignore them. He learned well, and from those first few years on the ice, Wayne was on the road to fame.

In 1977 he moved to Sault Ste. Marie, Ontario, to live with family friends while he played his first full year at the top level of junior hockey. At the tender age of 16, he wore the now-famous 99 on his hockey jersey for the first time and played for the Sault Ste. Marie Greyhounds with all the energy he had put into practices on his small backyard rink. His 70 goals during the year earned him the Ontario Hockey Association's Rookie of the Year Award and brought him to the attention of the World Hockey Association's (WHA) Indianapolis Racers, who offered Gretzky his first professional contract on June 13, 1978.

Born on January 26, 1961, Wayne was technically too young to play on a professional team, but his agent, Gus Badali, argued that he be given a chance. At 17, Wayne Gretzky became the youngest player in professional hockey and likely one of the youngest people in Canada at the time with a sports contract worth $875,000. Sadly for the Racers, but luckily for Canada, Gretzky was sold to the rival Edmonton Oilers in November 1978 after only eight games. It was not Gretzky's playing that prompted the move, but financial trouble within the Indianapolis franchise.

Back home in Canada, Gretzky continued his phenomenal playing, scoring 46 goals and winning the league's 1978–79 Rookie of the Year Award at 18 years of age. The highlight of Gretzky's playing year, however, was neither the high goal count nor the award. On January 5, 1979, three weeks shy of his 18th birthday, Gretzky joined Gordie Howe on the WHA all-star team to play against the Dynamos from Moscow. The young player had fulfilled his dream of one day sharing the ice with his hero.

With the demise of the WHA, the Edmonton Oilers became part of the National Hockey League (NHL), and rumours and sports bar bets began flying. The NHL had a reputation for being a physically brutal environment. There was speculation among players and fans alike that Gretzky, young and comparatively small, would never stand up to the aggressive stick-handling, severe cross-checking and high-velocity passing that took place on NHL ice. How wrong they were!

Accustomed to dealing with bigger, more aggressive players all along, Gretzky simply used his strategic game to confound everyone—except Gretzky himself. When responding to questions about his secret, he might just as easily have been explaining strategy in a game of chess or billiards. His biographer Josh Wilker quotes Gretzky as saying: "The whole sport is angles and caroms [rebounds], forgetting the straight direction the puck is going, calculating where it will be diverted, factoring in all the interruptions. Basically, my whole game is angles."

Gretzky, who had dropped out of high school before graduating in order to follow his dream career, was gaining phenomenal success from applied mathematics. The countless hours spent on that little backyard rink in Brantford were reaping rewards. Gretzky's astounding ability to determine precisely where the puck would end up allowed him to be there to meet it when it was passed by someone else, and to pass it to teammates with eye-popping accuracy. He didn't need to out skate or brutalize the opposition. He simply outmanoeuvred them. Nor did he have to intimidate others with pucks delivered at lethal velocity. Word around the arenas was that Gretzky's shots were fired so softly you could catch them with your bare hands—if you could just figure out when, and from where, the amazing centre was going to launch them.

For the next eight years, from 1980 through 1988, Gretzky remained with the Edmonton Oilers, winning the NHL Hart Trophy as most valuable player every year, and the Art Ross Trophy for the league's leading scorer six years in a row, from 1980 through 1986. During his time with the Oilers, he became the opposition goalie's worst nightmare, holding the puck as he did for a tortuously long time in front of the opposing net.

He helped the Oilers win the Stanley Cup four times and Team Canada win the Canada Cup in 1984 and again in 1987. During the 1986–87 season, when he was 25, he reached 500 career goals, the youngest player in the history of the game to do so. In 1987 he became the all-time leading Stanley Cup scorer, with 177 career points, topping legend Jean Beliveau. In March 1988 he surpassed his idol, Gordie Howe, to earn hockey's record for most assists—1050.

On August 9, 1988, fans all over Canada mourned when it was announced that Gretzky had been traded to the Los Angeles Kings. What was agony for Canadian hockey became an ecstasy for southern California. In 1988 the Los Angeles Kings were struggling to lure fans to games. Gretzky changed all that. In his first season with the Kings, the team achieved the most improved record in the NHL, coming second in the Smythe Division, and Gretzky picked up his ninth Hart Trophy. On October 15, 1989, he scored his 1851st career point, once more surpassing Gordie Howe's record. California fans began flocking to games. In 1991 the Los Angeles Kings were the only southern California team to sell out every single home game. Fans were coming to watch the Great One play. But suddenly it looked as though it might all be over.

In spring 1992, Gretzky, at 31, was suffering from a herniated thoracic disk in his back, a painful and disabling condition that threatened to keep him off the ice for at least a year. But his amazing powers of will and determination won out. After only eight months of rest and recuperation, Gretzky returned to centre ice and helped take the Kings to their first and only Stanley Cup. Gretzky was back, with even more steam than before. In 1993–94, the year following his return to the ice, he earned the Art Ross Trophy as the league's leading scorer for the 10th time. He was also awarded the Lady Byng Memorial Trophy for sportsmanship for the fourth time, following up on previous selection for the award in 1980 with the Oilers, and 1991 and 1992 with the Kings. The next year he moved once more, this time to the St. Louis Blues. But at the end of the season he left St. Louis to join the New York Rangers as a free agent. There he was able to work with friend and former teammate Mark Messier for one season before Messier moved to the Vancouver Canucks in 1997.

In 1998 Gretzky competed for Canada at the Olympic Winter Games in Nagano, Japan, but he still had a few more goals to make in New York. He continued to top his own records in goals and assists for the three years he played with the Rangers, becoming the all-time leading scorer in NHL all-star game history during a 1998 game in Vancouver, and finishing the 1999 season with 894 goals and 1963 assists.

On April 16, 1999, after 20 seasons of outstanding playing and just weeks after scoring his 1072th career goal (including goals scored in the playoffs and the WHA), surpassing Gordie Howe's long-standing record, Wayne Gretzky announced his retirement. Honours poured in, including the unique distinction of having his number 99 retired from all NHL teams. That year the *Hockey News* named him the greatest player in NHL history. In November 1999, Gretzky was inducted into the Canadian Hockey Hall of Fame in Toronto, and in

December the same year, ESPN named Gretzky one of the five greatest athletes of the 20th century.

Gretzky retired to enjoy a well-deserved rest with his wife Janet, a former California actress, and their five children. But kudos and retirement did not mean that Wayne Gretzky turned his back on his beloved game. He continues to support hockey and youth in various ways: the Wayne Gretzky Foundation provides equipment and coaching to allow youth from disadvantaged backgrounds to play hockey; he was manager of Canada's men's hockey team for the 2002 Winter Olympics and for the 2004 World Cup of Hockey. The Wayne Gretzky Fantasy Camp, which held its first session in 2003, helps youngsters improve their skills with coaching from famous pro hockey players. In addition to his charity and foundation work, Wayne Gretzky has become a well-known face off the ice as spokesperson for a number of high-profile products, from automobiles to soft drinks and breakfast cereal.

Although Wayne Gretzky is likely earning more money for his endorsements alone than most people will earn in their lifetimes, not many will resent him for it. He has been a positive and significant role model for thousands of Canadian youngsters. Throughout his playing career, Wayne Gretzky epitomized sportsmanship, sport's most sought-after characteristic. Despite the threatening howls of irate and envious parents when he was a kid and the aggressive wrestling-ring tactics of less able players in the NHL, Wayne Gretzky managed to maintain his reputation as a gentleman, winning the Lady Byng Memorial Trophy, the NHL's prize for sportsmanlike conduct, five times. An outstanding athlete, a generous mentor for young players, and a hockey player who succeeded through skill and intelligence, Wayne Gretzky is truly a great Canadian.

CHAPTER FIVE

Sir John A. Macdonald
(1815–1891)

*Be philosophical, and if Fortune empties a chamber
pot on your head, just smile and say, 'We are having
a summer shower.'*

–Sir John A. Macdonald

JOHN A. MACDONALD WAS NEITHER ANGEL NOR MADMAN,
although he was, at various times during his life,
characterized as both. His political career was
marred by controversy and scandal, and his personal life was saddened by loneliness and tragedy.
But he rose above it all to be remembered as the
man who unified Canada and became the Dominion's first prime minister.

He was born in Scotland on January 10, 1815,
but his life influences came primarily from the
new land to which his parents, Hugh and Helen
Macdonald, immigrated in 1820 with their two
sons and two daughters. They settled in the
Kingston area of Upper Canada, some 300 kilometres from Toronto, where Hugh attempted to earn
a livelihood at a variety of retail businesses. Proud
people with high ambitions for their bright and
studious eldest son, the elder Macdonalds didn't

have the wealth necessary to send John to university. At 15, with as much schooling as was then necessary to become a student at law, young John became an apprentice in the law office of a Kingston lawyer who was a friend of the family.

Within a short time, John began running, with admirable organization and maturity, his mentor's branch office in the neighbouring town of Napanee. He quickly established a good reputation among colleagues in the legal community. When he was called to the bar in 1836 at the age of 21, he received encouragement and support that enabled him to set up his own law practice in Kingston.

From the start it was clear that young John Macdonald was set for success. He could never have been called handsome, for his nose was long enough to later provide decades of fodder for political cartoonists. But he was tall and lean, with piercing blue eyes, a quick and mischievous sense of humour and a solid understanding of the law of the land. Most beneficial of all in that place and time, he came from a staunch Scottish Protestant background. His law practice prospered.

In 1842, he made his first trip back to Scotland and England, partly to settle some business affairs that lingered after his father's death in 1841 and partly to recover from several months of ill health. John's health made a drastic improvement while he was abroad. The recovery may have been due to the well-prepared hotel meals, which must have been a particular delight for a bachelor who had been living alone, or to the excitement he derived from attending lively debates at the British Houses of Parliament. Or his improved state of health may have been attributed to his falling in love.

Her name was Isabella Clark, and she was the poised and charming stepdaughter of one of his uncles. John, 27, was smitten with the 33-year-old Isa, and it appears the feeling was mutual. Just over one year later, Isa sailed to Kingston, where the couple was married on September 1, 1843.

John's interest in politics had been whetted when the 1841 Act of Union merged Upper and Lower Canada to create the Province of Canada, which was subdivided into Canada East and Canada West. The capital of the new province was Kingston. His political enthusiasm was further piqued in England. When his friends urged him to run for election as a Kingston alderman in 1843, he did. With his excellent support and fine reputation, it was no surprise that he won. It was also no surprise to Isa when, in 1844, her young husband came home with the news that he had decided to run for the provincial parliament in the next general election.

Macdonald was again successful, entering provincial politics as a moderate Conservative. The seat of parliament had been moved to Montréal,

120 kilometres from Kingston, and Macdonald was religious in his attendance at sessions. He soon became widely respected for his witty, incisive comments, which were tempered by a somewhat contemplative reaction time, a characteristic that was later to be viewed as the vice of indecision. His side-by-side professional careers of law and politics were thriving, but his wife's health was not.

In the autumn of 1845, Macdonald took Isa to the southern United States for an extended recuperative stay in Georgia, managing to visit with her for several weeks at a time over the next two years. In May 1847, John was named receiver-general. Three months later their son was born, leaving Isa's health even more delicate.

In March 1848, Macdonald's political future suddenly looked precarious when the Conservative government fell after a non-confidence vote. Overnight, Macdonald was a member of the opposition. That August, Isa returned to Kingston with their one-year-old baby. Macdonald was named Queen's Counsel, and he might have been content to simply run his law firm and take care of his sickly wife and their new son, but it would not be that easy. Alexander Campbell, Macdonald's law partner, had become increasingly frustrated with having to run the practice alone while Macdonald was off making a name for himself in politics. Shortly after Isa returned, Campbell broke up the partnership, leaving Macdonald bitter and scrambling to keep his practice operating at a profit. And profit he badly needed.

Believing that the quiet of the country might improve Isa's health, he moved the family to Bellevue House, a small villa decorated in a unique and ornate style that caused Macdonald to nickname it the Pekoe Pagoda. Despite the whimsical nickname, Macdonald's life in that house was not a happy one. Their baby son died at the age of 13 months, and even though Isabella gave birth to another son in 1850, she never regained her health. Macdonald hired servants to help in the home and did everything he could to keep his wife healthy. But she continued to decline, spending most of her time in bed or in a wheelchair. For solace, Macdonald turned to the bottle.

Despite his personal hardships and occasional alcoholic lapses, Macdonald continued to do well on the political scene. He acquired a new law partner, which gave him more time to spend on political matters. In 1854, with the Conservatives back in power, Macdonald became attorney general. The following year he met George-Étienne Cartier, a corporate lawyer from Montréal and a moderate Conservative. With similar interests and political views, they became close friends.

As the government's most senior member, John Macdonald became premier in 1857 when Conservative leader Allan MacNab resigned. Macdonald immediately named Cartier as co-leader of the party. In the general election that followed, Macdonald won his seat, as did Cartier.

A few months later, on December 28, 1857, just months after the Macdonalds' son Hugh John celebrated his seventh birthday, Isabella died. As if being left a widower and a single father was not enough, there was political unrest brewing, particularly in Canada West. Representation by population, the controversial "rep by pop" that had been loudly demanded by Canada West Liberals, was creating a difficulty for Macdonald and his Conservatives. Canada West felt entitled to more elected representatives than the now less-populated Canada East, and factions from both sides, in an attempt to show strength, made all governmental decisions as difficult as possible. Macdonald's bouts with alcohol became more frequent and more severe, but they did not prevent him from doing his job. He set up departments of fisheries, agriculture and military affairs, and ensured budget decisions were made in a fiscally responsible manner.

In an interesting political move of 1858, which the media aptly named "the Double Shuffle," Macdonald showed he was not above some sleight of hand to keep his government together. One of the issues over which Canada East and Canada West argued was the location of the seat of government. Canada East wanted Québec City; Canada West wanted Toronto. Macdonald left the decision up to Queen Victoria, who chose Ottawa.

Dissatisfied with Her Majesty's decision, members from both sides voted the government down. In response, Macdonald and Cartier resigned, allowing the Liberals to form the government. It was a brilliant and calculated move. Liberal leader George Brown was forced to call an election, and he and his ministers had to return to their constituencies to be voted back into office. In their absence, Macdonald and his Conservatives defeated them and took control of the government once more.

Macdonald and Cartier led the government of the Province of Canada for the next four years, but were defeated in May 1862. The defeat was principally the result of the failure of the Militia Bill, which the Conservatives attempted to pass in an effort to build the Canadian military.

In April 1864, Macdonald and his Conservatives were once more voted into power, and then out again in June of the same year. They spent the remainder of 1864 working up to the Charlottetown Conference, which took place in September, and then the Quebec Conference in October. The conferences' success in laying the groundwork and creating the documents that led to Confederation was largely due to Macdonald's insight and vision. Further progress followed a courageous move by George Brown and his fellow Liberals, who offered Macdonald and his Conservatives an opportunity to form a coalition government. It was a credit to all concerned that they accepted.

The British North America (BNA) Act, which established the new Dominion of Canada—made up of Ontario (formerly Canada West), Québec (formerly Canada East), New Brunswick and Nova Scotia—was given final approval by Britain and became law in 1867. Macdonald, who had become the senior member of the coalition government on George Brown's resignation in 1865, was named leader of the new Dominion. For his efforts in the formation of the fledgling country, the 52-year-old politician was knighted.

Sir John A. Macdonald, the first prime minister of Canada, presided over festivities to celebrate the birth of the new nation on that first Dominion Day, July 1, 1867. It was a momentous occasion for Macdonald, made all the more happy because he once again had a woman he loved by his side. While in London the previous year for discussions about the BNA Act, Macdonald had met a lovely woman named Susan Agnes Bernard (1836–1920), who was the sister of his personal secretary. Some months before his appointment as prime minister, Macdonald had married Agnes, and his personal life seemed settled. The new Lady Macdonald (Baroness Macdonald of Earnscliffe) was a good choice as a prime minister's wife. She was intelligent but not overbearing, sociable but always appropriately reserved, a loyal supporter of his ideas, but someone Macdonald could count on to give her own opinion. Sadly, their solid relationship did not shield them from tragedy.

In 1869, two years into his term, Macdonald discovered that his law practice was bankrupt. His second partner, A.J. MacDonnell, who died in 1864, had been a good lawyer but a poor businessman. Debts he had accumulated, both personally and on behalf of the firm, had gradually grown over the years when Macdonald's attention was on the future of the nation. By the time Macdonald became aware of the situation, his law firm had debts in excess of its value. Forced to mortgage his home and his business, 54-year-old Macdonald found it necessary to start over financially. But money was not his only anguish at that time.

Agnes gave birth to their daughter, Mary, on February 15, 1869. The child seemed normal at the beginning, but it soon became apparent that all was not well. Little Mary was found to be physically and mentally disabled and spent the rest of her long life (she died in 1933) in a wheelchair, totally dependent on others for comfort and survival. It was a severe blow to Macdonald, who was extremely fond of his little girl. Once again, he took comfort in alcohol. About to be confronted with the most significant decision of his political career, Macdonald's subsequent missteps were entirely predictable.

One of Macdonald's goals was to bring the West into Confederation. His first target was the Red River Settlement in the Hudson's Bay Company's territory known as Rupert's Land. In the first of several poor decisions, Macdonald appointed a lieutenant-governor without consulting the Métis, the majority population in the area. To show their dissatisfaction with the treatment, the Métis, led by Louis Riel, set up a provisional government and drew up a list of clauses they wished to include in any talks about joining Canada.

Macdonald made a quick but temporary save by negotiating with Riel and his followers. Canada accepted the terms of the Manitoba Act and welcomed Manitoba into Confederation in July 1870, giving Métis control over their language and their religion. But in laying the foundations for the new province, Riel had overseen the court martial and subsequent execution of Thomas Scott, a violent and bigoted protester against Métis control of Red River. Macdonald branded Riel a traitor and exiled him to the United States. Macdonald had effectively pushed the Métis demands into the background, hoping the problem would work itself out. This was typical of Macdonald's method of operating, which had earned him the nickname "Old Tomorrow." It was a move that was to come back to haunt him.

Meanwhile, Macdonald was busy bringing British Columbia on board. After some preliminary talks and amicable negotiations, he realized his goal. On July 20, 1871, British Columbia became the sixth province to enter Confederation. With the dream of a coast-to-coast nation now a reality, Macdonald set about the construction of the

Canadian Pacific Railway (CPR), a project that was one of the terms of British Columbia's entry into the union. It was a well-supported project and a necessary one, but the "Pacific Scandal" that erupted over the building of the CPR led to the prime minister's first major defeat.

With the 1872 election looming and his own financial condition in a disastrous state, Sir John made an ill-advised decision to accept funds from a private individual, who raised substantial amounts of money to support Macdonald's campaign and subsequent re-election. Shortly after the announcement was made in 1873 that the CPR project was going through as planned, all hell broke loose. It was discovered that the contract for building the massive rail line that would stretch "a mari usque ad mare" ("from sea even unto sea"—Canada's motto) had been conferred on none other than Sir Hugh Allan, the individual who had financed Macdonald's successful campaign the year before. In the resulting backlash, which uncovered widespread voter payoffs, many of Macdonald's colleagues withdrew their support. Without the wise counsel of his friend George-Étienne Cartier, who had died a few months earlier, Macdonald was alone. On November 5, 1873, he resigned as prime minister, and Alexander Mackenzie took over the government.

In the subsequent election called in early 1874, Mackenzie and the Liberals won an easy victory. At 67, Macdonald was out of the prime minister's office and effectively out of a salary. He took a brief hiatus, during which he decided to stay on as Conservative leader. It was a good decision.

The Liberal government made sweeping reforms to the country's election procedures. To prevent the kind of coercion and bribery that had taken place during the Pacific Scandal, they put in place a secret ballot and standards that would ensure such an incident never occurred again. Liberal support was growing by the day. But Macdonald bided his time, curbing his tongue as leader of the opposition when the Liberals passed the Canadian Temperance Act of 1878. Old Tomorrow's habit of waiting until things sorted themselves out finally paid off. For personal and democratic reasons, he was against the adoption of a law that would give each jurisdiction control over its liquor laws. As it turned out, the act was so unfavourably received by the Canadian public that the Liberals were defeated in the 1878 general election. Sir John A. was once again the country's prime minister. But he had a tough few years ahead of him.

Severe droughts, crop failure and human disease had been plaguing the aboriginal and Métis residents of Manitoba and the territory between the Red River and the Rockies that later became Saskatchewan and Alberta. In 1884 the beleaguered people, unable to get any practical assistance from Ottawa, and their claims for promised land consistently ignored, begged Louis Riel to return to

Canada from the United States to help them. He set up a provisional government at Batoche, Saskatchewan, in March 1885. Macdonald, who was the minister responsible for Indian Affairs and for the Interior as well as prime minister, sent about 5000 hastily assembled troops and the North-West Mounted Police (NWMP) to quell the rebellion. After several skirmishes, Louis Riel surrendered on May 15, 1885, and was convicted of treason. Wishing once and for all to rid himself of this rebel, Macdonald ignored a recommendation for clemency from the sympathetic jury, and Riel was hanged for treason. (For a more complete account of the Northwest Rebellion, please see Chapter Ten on Louis Riel.)

There was immediate and negative reaction in many parts of the country, particularly in Québec and the West. But a quick cabinet shuffle, which placed the most diplomatic ministers in strategic positions, calmed the waters. The voters returned the Conservatives to power for another two terms, the second of which saw the prime minister's son, Hugh John Macdonald, elected to the House of Commons as the representative for Winnipeg. Hugh later followed in his father's footsteps as minister of the Interior.

Sir John A. Macdonald did not live to see his son become premier of Manitoba for one year in 1900. He suffered a stroke in May 1891 and died less than one month later on June 6, 1891. He was 76. He did live long enough to see the Canada he had dreamed about, united from Atlantic to Pacific, its resources and industry protected by tariffs, its people protected by the NWMP—all of these a fitting legacy to John A. Macdonald's more than 50 years of service to his country.

CHAPTER SIX

Nellie McClung
(1873–1951)

Women are going to form a chain, a greater sister-hood than the world has ever known.

–Nellie McClung

THERE ARE CURRENTLY 33 WOMEN IN THE CANADIAN SENATE, and 65 of 391 members of the House of Commons are women. Of the Fortune 500 companies operating in the world today, eight have women at the helm, there are female presidents at three of the top five universities in the country. Those who realize just how much women's lives have improved since the turn of the 20th century have people like Nellie McClung to thank.

"Our Nellie," as she became known to later generations of proud Western Canadians, was born Helen (Nellie) Letitia Mooney on October 20, 1873, in Grey County, Ontario. She was the youngest of six children born to John Mooney, an Irish immigrant, and his Scottish-born wife, Letitia.

At age six, Nellie was uprooted from her simple but comfortable farm home and moved to the vast Manitoba prairie. Her father, then 68, and her

47-year-old mother had answered the call of the
West, with its stories of rich, fertile soil and wide
open spaces. Hoping to establish a better legacy for
their maturing family, they accepted the Canadian
government's offer of cheap land.

The trek west to their home on the prairies was
not an easy one. By the time the Mooney family
settled in their chosen locale near the town of Millford (now Wawanesa), nearly 12 months had
passed. The year had been a hard but particularly
interesting one for little Nellie. A bright, inquisitive
and active child, she noticed everything and
quickly developed opinions about what she experienced. As the youngest of a sizeable family, she
was somewhat doted on. She nevertheless learned
early about the difficulties of rural life, particularly
for women. She was later able to turn her experiences into wonderful stories that played up the
joys of homesteading life. But for the present,
there was work to do.

The Mooney family soon discovered that the
rich, fertile soil promised them was actually heavy,
clay-laden Manitoba gumbo, which built up on the
soles of their boots after rains, then set like con-
crete when dry. They learned that the clean, clear
air, far away from factory smoke, was an ideal
breeding ground for mosquitoes in summer and
marauding grasshoppers in fall. They found that
their arid and windblown prairie home could be
quickly inundated with floodwaters from the
swollen Souris River in spring. In winter, when

the thermometer made its first plunge to −50°C, they discovered an entirely new concept of cold. But there were compensations.

The bushes in the fields surrounding their thatched-roof house were heavy with wild berries that made their way into delicious pies and home-made jams; the fields of grain supplied flour for golden, butter-crusted bread; and the clean fresh air made for quick drying time on laundry day. There were country fairs, picnics and communal barn raisings. Although the Mooney children didn't have many luxuries, they enjoyed a com-fortable and happy home life, thanks to their hard-working, God-fearing parents, who raised them with an admirable work ethic.

Nellie, taught to read by her older sisters, was an avid reader and writer even before her first experiences at the nearby Northfield schoolhouse. It wasn't long before Nellie was writing stories about her life. As she wrote, she thought more about it—the joys, the beauty of nature, but also the hardships. With an inquisitiveness that some-times frustrated her teachers and family alike, she began questioning why girls, who worked every bit as hard as boys on the farm, were not allowed to play when their tasks were done. She won-dered why her brothers could spend their leisure time at fun pursuits like stickball and marbles, while she and her older sisters, Hannah and Lizzie, were expected to relax by mending socks and stitching bed linens.

Nellie, of course, was viewing life from a child's point of view and perhaps failed to understand the practicalities of such a structure. Farm life was hard on both men and women unless they were wealthy enough to hire someone else to do chores. They often had to take care of their homes and property without the aid of machinery and without electricity. Fields were harrowed and seeded with horse-drawn equipment and harvested by hand.

Laundry was done by women, their reddened hands scrubbing soiled, rough garments over a washboard using strong, homemade lye soap. Men chopped wood for the stoves to stoke the fires that women used to bake bread and boil soup. Wells had to be dug and water hauled to the house on a daily basis, and animals had to be fenced in and fed. Kitchen gardens had to be tilled and planted, weeded and harvested, their yield blanched and bottled or buried in huge sand-filled vats for use in winter. There were customary jobs for each gender, but roles were reversed or shared when necessity demanded it, although it was often women who helped the men do their jobs—rarely the other way around.

There were no department stores in rural areas, and catalogue items were too expensive for most people, so clothes were handmade and then altered to fit subsequent wearers. As a result of the hardships of everyday life, it was not unusual for young people to be kept home from school to help with chores. The inequalities in this again struck Nellie. At this time in history, men were in most leadership positions—they were the doctors, lawyers, politicians. It was widely accepted that young men required education and young women did not, so a family made every effort to ensure its sons went to school. As a daughter, Nellie was frequently kept home from school to help with the never-ending work. After her two older sisters left home, it became even worse.

By the time Nellie was 15, she had spent less than five years in a schoolroom, but it was about this time that her sisters became her mentors. Her sister Hannah had trained as a teacher and was working near Brandon, Manitoba. She and Lizzie offered to pay Nellie's way when, in 1889, Nellie passed the examinations that allowed her to train as a teacher in Winnipeg.

Although not far away by present-day standards, Winnipeg was a world removed from tiny Millford. A thriving metropolis in 1889, Winnipeg was at the crossroads of the nation, a hub of rail activity that carried goods from the four corners of the continent. There were streetcars and ten-storey buildings on bustling Portage Avenue. On Main Street there were department stores selling furs and high-buttoned boots, and street vendors hawked delectable hot, roasted chestnuts and questionable remedies for chilblains. There were skating rinks in winter and flower-filled parks in summer.

Despite the potential for distraction, young Nellie worked hard at the Winnipeg Normal School. She was 16 when she completed the five-month teacher-training program and was offered her first teaching job at the one-room schoolhouse in Somerset, Manitoba, a village 70 kilometres southwest of Winnipeg. She was a successful teacher, entertaining her students with her somewhat embellished stories and flouting convention by taking them on field trips. Her excellent rapport with the children did not go unnoticed by one of the school trustees, who hired Nellie the following year to teach in his hometown of Manitou, Manitoba.

Nellie decided to accept an invitation to board at the home of the local parson and his wife, a couple Nellie had met at church. It was a pivotal decision in her life. The couple, the McClungs, had a son, Wes, who was just two years older than Nellie. Nellie had met Wes earlier and liked him. He was bright and good-looking and seemed to share the Christian values Nellie had grown up with. The two young people spent many hours together under the watchful, but always hopeful, eye of Wes's mother.

Mrs. McClung herself came to have an influence on Nellie's life that had nothing whatever to do with her smitten son. A lively and forward-looking woman, the middle-aged parson's wife was an active and dedicated member of the Women's

Christian Temperance Union (WCTU). The group was originally established to end the family problems caused by over-consumption of alcohol. But it had, since its inception in Ohio in 1874, taken on battles against other social ills. Recognizing strong moral character and a support of family values and social justice in Methodist-reared Nellie, Mrs. McClung recruited her young friend into the organization.

When Nellie upgraded her teaching credentials in 1893, she was assigned to a larger school, this time in Treherne, Manitoba, some 50 kilometres from Manitou. While in Treherne, Nellie continued her friendship with Wes and his mother. She also joined the local branch of the WCTU, becoming a member of the board when she was just 21 years old. Her training as a schoolteacher gave her a unique ability to teach the younger generation about the dangers of the demon rum, and she made use of every opportunity to do so.

In September 1894, Wes went off to study at the University of Toronto, and the two young people had to continue their relationship through letters. When Wes graduated in 1896 with a degree in pharmacy, they married and moved to Manitou, where Wes bought and ran the town's drugstore.

The young McClungs' first child, Jack, was born on June 16, 1897, and was followed by Florence in 1899 and Paul in 1901. Married life and subsequent motherhood did not dampen Nellie's enthusiasm or energy for her work with the WCTU. With three small children at home, she was no longer teaching, but the public speaking skills she had developed were of great benefit to the WCTU. She began addressing small groups and soon had invitations to speak from all over the area. In 1907 she was keynote speaker at the WCTU provincial convention. The response to her speeches was so enthusiastic that she realized this was what she had been born to do.

Public speaking was not her only talent. As a young girl on the farm, Nellie had found writing to be a particularly pleasant pastime. She wrote poetry and stories as well as diaries of everyday events. While her generous and supportive mother-in-law took care of the children, who soon numbered four, Nellie McClung wrote and accepted invitations to speak on behalf of the WCTU—invitations that were now coming from all over Manitoba. Both endeavours were successful. Nellie's speeches raised the profile of the WCTU, and in 1908 her first book, *Sowing Seeds in Danny*, was published, followed by *The Second Chance* in 1910. Both novels, with their somewhat romanticized depiction of prairie homesteading, were extremely popular. The first book became a Canadian bestseller and earned 35-year-old Nellie $25,000, a considerable amount of money for that time.

Although Nellie loved her life in Manitou, she happily moved the family to Winnipeg in 1911 when Wes sold the pharmacy to take a position with Manufacturers Life Insurance. Nellie was aware of the WCTU's high level of activity in Winnipeg. She was also aware of how needed it was.

Small towns, certainly small towns of the past, served a certain censorship function on the lives of residents. Everyone usually knew who were the hard-drinking men and who were the ones likely to take out their drunken frustrations on their innocent families. Clergymen and the WCTU alike were aware of which families needed their help, and they knew precisely which establishments catered to these men.

The mighty metropolis of Winnipeg was different. Breweries abounded and so did bars, pubs and beverage rooms. Most residents would have to walk no farther than three blocks in any direction to find a drink.

In Winnipeg, Nellie was delighted to come into contact with the Canadian Women's Press Club. As women who held responsible jobs outside their homes, Press Club members were able to introduce Nellie to some of the discrimination they saw against women. On the one hand, women were not allowed to vote because they were not considered responsible, yet on the other hand, they were responsible enough to be punished for their crimes. Just 12 years earlier, in 1899, 21-year-old Hilda

Blake of Brandon was hanged for the murder of her employer. The memory of that young woman's final and hopeless goodbye haunted Nellie.

Because women were not permitted to vote, legislation to protect women in the workforce and at home was either poor or non-existent. Many politicians viewed women who worked outside the home to be less than serious workers. Manitoba premier Rodmond Roblin believed that such women worked for "pin" money. Sadly, many women felt the same way. There was a social stigma against women working outside the home, and rather than rallying to help others combat the cycle, many women looked down on the very ones in their group who defied custom. The general feeling, hinted at in fairly subtle ways, was that a women should be smart enough to marry well so that her husband would take care of her, thus maintaining the social order. As a result of these views, the workplace was not only unwelcoming to women, but was also often brutal. Most working women held menial jobs and received minimal pay. They spent their working hours in deplorable conditions, had no access to benefits of any kind and were often let go without notice or reason.

In 1912, Nellie published her third book, *The Black Creek Stopping-House*. Its sales permitted Nellie to hire help at home, giving her more time to campaign for her causes. She and her fellow writers at the Press Club saw that reform was required, and they attempted to achieve it on three general levels. They wanted to convince men that women were capable, to encourage women to test their limits, and to challenge existing legislation to improve the lives of women. They realized that legislation would be changed only if women had a voice. Women would have to gain the right to vote.

Impatient with Roblin's attitude toward the plight of working women, which alternated between annoyance and paternalism, Nellie McClung led a spinoff group of six club members, the Winnipeg Political Equality League (WPEL), to push the political agenda. They made the vote for women their goal, and Premier Roblin their prime target. They pressed him with statistics and details. They hounded him with letters and visits. They arranged for him to visit a garment factory, where Roblin witnessed for himself the deplorable conditions. Still, he continued to resist pressure to do anything about it.

Unable to convince the premier, the group decided its only hope was to work for his defeat in the next election. The WPEL put on a satirical play in which Nellie took the role of Roblin, mimicking his speech and mocking his political stance in commendable comedic style. The play, entitled *The Woman's Parliament,* was a hit. Although Roblin's Conservative government was re-elected in 1914, people were beginning to rally to the cause of women thanks to the efforts of Nellie and her fellow suffragists.

Demand for improvements in workplace conditions intensified with the advent of World War I.
Factories sprang up in support of the war effort,
and since most of the men were overseas, women
were needed for the work. Women who had pre-
viously scoffed at the idea of working were themselves now part of the workforce.

The war and the public's increased awareness
created a shift in the political tides. Roblin's Conservative government went down to defeat in 1915.
The Liberals, vocal supporters of women's suffrage,
took power and on January 27, 1916, legislated
women's right to vote in Manitoba's provincial
elections. Within weeks, the government passed
the Manitoba Temperance Act, which prohibited
the sale of alcohol other than in pharmacies, where
sales would require a doctor's prescription.

Nellie and her colleagues had won two battles in
their war, but Nellie did not remain in Manitoba to
exercise the vote she had worked so hard to win.
In autumn 1914, Wes was transferred to the
Edmonton office of his insurance company, and
Nellie helped him pack up and move west with a
family that had expanded to five children, four
boys and one girl, ranging in age from 4 to 17.

In Edmonton, Nellie picked up the fight for suffrage and temperance, resuming a heavy schedule of speaking engagements and committee
work. With a well-employed husband who was
consistently supportive of her work, Nellie, at 41,

NELLIE MCCLUNG   71

could leave her children and home in the care of paid help while she pursued her interests. But her smooth domestic situation never blinded her to the realities of life for the majority of women she encountered. Most of her speaking engagements reflected this sensitivity, and Nellie rarely, if ever, charged for her words of wisdom. She continued to write as well, and by the time the war ended she had published one more novel and two essay collections.

Her political career up to this time had largely been one of activism, writing and committee work. In 1921 she was elected as a Liberal member of the Alberta legislature, and for the next four years she worked to liberalize birth control, revamp property rights to ensure security for women in the event of divorce, improve family allowances and health care and prohibit sales of alcohol. She was not re-elected for a second term, and there was speculation that hotel owners had waged a quiet but effective campaign to get rid of the voice that was keeping liquor out of their hotels and money out of their pockets. But Nellie was about to enter what was perhaps the most significant battle of her career.

While Nellie had been busy writing, raising her family and pursuing lofty ideals, another leading woman of the time, Judge Alice Jamieson, was fighting a public battle with a disgruntled defence attorney, John Cameron, who was dissatisfied with the way in which Jamieson had handled a case. In 1876, the judge hearing the case of an Englishwoman who had been arrested for voting had ruled that women were not persons in matters of rights and privileges. That ruling was still in effect throughout the Commonwealth. Cameron attempted to have Jamieson removed from her position as magistrate, arguing that she was not a person and therefore could not act as a judge.

The Provincial Court of Alberta heard Cameron's application to have her removed, and on November 26, 1917, the justices declared there was "no legal disqualification for holding public office in the government of the country [Alberta] arising from any distinction of sex."

With that decision, Alice Jamieson was legally declared a person. The decision was valid only in Alberta, but it kindled a fire in Nellie McClung and other women across the country. They pushed for the Canadian legal system to follow Alberta's precedent and declare women as persons under the law right across the country.

Finally, Nellie and four other women—Emily Murphy, Henrietta Edwards, Louise McKinney and Irene Parlby—who became known as the Famous Five, appealed to the Supreme Court of Canada to clarify if women were considered persons. The Supreme Court ruled against them, but their subsequent appeal to the Judicial Committee of the British Privy Council, the highest court available to interpret constitutional matters, was successful. On October 18, 1929, the Judicial Committee ruled that Canadian women were, in fact, persons with all the rights and privileges personhood permitted.

When the McClungs moved to Victoria in 1935 after Wes retired, Nellie began writing her memoirs. The first volume of the autobiography, *Clearing in the West*, was published in 1935. Although she focused largely on her writing in her later years, Nellie remained active with the Canadian Women's Press Club and the Canadian Authors Association, adding cultural nationalism to her long list of causes.

In 1936 she became the first woman member of the CBC board of governors, and in 1938 she was the only woman on the Canadian delegation to the League of Nations in Geneva, Switzerland. She continued to write articles and short stories and the second volume of her memoirs, *The Stream Runs Fast*, which was published in 1945.

Nellie McClung died at her home in Victoria on September 1, 1951, at the age of 77. She was surrounded by her family and mourned by the nation that had benefited so greatly from her energy, her vision and her sense of justice.

A monument entitled *Women are Persons!*, the work of Edmonton artist Barbara Paterson, was unveiled on Parliament Hill in Ottawa in October 2000 to commemorate Nellie McClung and the other members of the Famous Five—women who made possible many of the legal rights and freedoms Canadian women enjoy today.

CHAPTER SEVEN

Marshall McLuhan
(1911–1980)

You mean my fallacy was all wrong?

– Marshall McLuhan

IT WAS A TIME IN CANADA'S HISTORY WHEN REVOLUTION—OF ideas, style, society and politics—was taking a firm grip on youth; an era in which television, the new medium, was opening up the world to us. This was the Canada that was suddenly and overwhelmingly confronted with the ideas of Marshall McLuhan. From the brilliant one-liners mimicked by pseudo-intellectual groupies, to the more serious theories that few understood, his ideas, by 1968, had certainly made the handsome, brilliant and enigmatic philosopher the darling of the free world.

Born in Edmonton, Alberta, on July 21, 1911, Herbert Marshall McLuhan was the eldest of two boys, the only children of Elsie and Herbert McLuhan. Shortly after the birth of his first son (called Marshall), Herbert, a quiet, unassuming and gentle man, went into real estate with three colleagues. They wanted to tap into the flourishing real estate market of pre-World War I Edmonton. When the real estate market crumbled three years later, bringing their business to financial collapse, Herbert reluctantly joined the army for what was to be a brief but thankfully uneventful stay. When his army stint was over, he and Elsie moved with Marshall and brother Maurice (b. 1913) to the thriving city of Winnipeg, where they settled in the midtown, middle-class neighbourhood of Fort Rouge.

Life was not all rosy for the McLuhan men. McLuhan biographer Philip Marchand character-izes Elsie as a vain, self-indulgent snob who thought that Winnipeg "represented the nadir of cultural life in Canada." Her unrelenting criticism of Herbert and their boring backwoods life was widely known in the community and sometimes embarrassed both husband and sons. But worse, and having more effect on her children, were her violent tirades and thinly disguised contempt for her husband.

Despite their volatile married life, both of McLuhan's parents influenced their elder son in ways that led to his success in later life. Elsie was a trained elocutionist who gave popular public readings and taught diction. From her, Marshall learned—if not formally, then certainly by exam-ple—to speak with crisp enunciation and also to withstand her pugnacious, sometimes vicious arguing. Their father, on the other hand, delighted in spending time with his sons, playing word games and telling them stories of his early life. When he was young, Marshall no doubt loved these times with his gentle father. Once he was enrolled at university, he became somewhat puffed up about being in an institution of higher learning and adopted his mother's disdain of Herbert, looking down on him for never having finished high school. It was behaviour that likely caused Marshall some remorse in his later life, when mellowness set in along with maturity. As Barrington Nevitt, McLuhan's long-time friend and collaborator notes: "Better than anyone else, Marshall [in his writing] reveals...how he grew up from a brash and opinionated young man to a witty and warm-hearted sage, who grew younger with age."

McLuhan liked university, although his enormous intellectual capacity did not manifest itself in top grades at the University of Manitoba, where he initially planned to study engineering. He found that he was mechanically challenged and switched concentrations to English and philosophy, disciplines more in keeping with his strong need for debate and verbal sparring.

In his third year, McLuhan became increasingly critical of both faculty and coursework at the university. He realized he was not being required to think but only study, accept and regurgitate currently held ideas. He was not achieving high marks, but his lack of respect for his professors made the poor grades something for him to shrug at rather than worry over. For his own part, McLuhan was determined to get an education, even if he had to do it himself. In addition to devising a number of strategies to help him remember what he read, he made it a goal to learn three new words each day. According to Philip Marchand, "He conceived the idea of listing important writers chronologically, accompanied by thumbnail sketches of their lives and works. For novels he wrote lists of characters with their roles in the narrative. For his readings in the *Reader's Digest*, he wrote a single brief comment at the end of interesting articles, developing his skill at concise summary."

He was continually thinking and questioning and was forever challenging others. It was a way of operating that forced him into a relatively barren social life. His relationships with fellow undergraduates tended to be based on ideas and issues rather than feelings. Even his leisure activities were more concentrated on specific goals than on leisure. Sailing on the Red River often became an examination of his perception of the size of objects as they receded into the distance; swimming and hockey were endured rather than enjoyed for their potential to bulk up his tall and very slender physique.

He derived his greatest enjoyment from debating. He could sometimes go on for hours, dancing nimbly from one side of the argument to another. He enjoyed this sparring even better when it was with someone whose mind approached his in agility. In McLuhan's opinion, that didn't happen often.

The lack of social life no doubt made it easier for McLuhan to concentrate on his studies. He earned his honours BA in 1933, developing along the way a fascination with Ezra Pound, James Joyce and English writers. The following summer he travelled to England with a university friend and became even more interested in things British. He returned to the University of Manitoba for graduate work, and in 1934, at age 23, he earned an MA in 18th-century English literature along with a provincial gold medal in English. Young McLuhan seemed to feel at home in England, so it was no surprise when he enrolled in Cambridge the autumn after his graduation to study English literature at its source, having secured a scholarship from the Imperial Order of Daughters of the Empire and a generous loan from his mother's sister Ethel.

McLuhan found himself humbled in the presence of the highly articulate students and the well-read and scholarly professors at Cambridge, and he lost a good deal of the superiority complex he had developed in Manitoba. He argued less and listened more and became particularly intrigued by the ideas of one professor, I.A. Richards. These ideas were the seeds that later grew into one of McLuhan's most famous premises: that a message is embedded in its context.

With his BA from Cambridge and his two degrees from Manitoba, McLuhan landed a position as a graduate teaching assistant in English at the University of Wisconsin in Madison. It was shortly after this move that McLuhan converted to Roman Catholicism. Raised in the Protestant tradition, McLuhan came to Catholicism after several years of considering the writings of G.K. Chesterton and after thoroughly examining his own system of beliefs. He was to remain a devout Catholic for the rest of his life, with a solid conviction that prayer and daily sacraments were the necessary means to a healthy relationship with his Creator.

With his conversion to Catholicism came a fervent desire to teach at a Catholic institution. In 1937 he accepted a teaching position in the English department at St. Louis University in Missouri. McLuhan seemed to blossom during his time in St. Louis. Meeting people who were his intellectual equals and who took ideas, but not themselves, seriously, he was able to relax somewhat while still enjoying countless intellectual sparring matches that were his life's blood.

It was at this time that he met the woman who would be his wife. Corinne Keller Lewis, a high school drama teacher, was a gracious and lovely southern belle from Fort Worth, Texas. After a somewhat trying long-distance courtship, they were married in a quick and simple ceremony during summer holidays in 1939. They went on a tour of Italy for their honeymoon and settled in Cambridge, England, where McLuhan had been accepted as a PhD student.

World War II did not have a detrimental effect on McLuhan's scholarly pursuits. He and Corinne lived a quiet, simple life that seemed to suit them both well. He was again among the ghosts he loved, the sages of Elizabethan England, and he had a beautiful, loyal and supportive woman by his side. It was a peaceful and productive time for them.

When his year of study was over, McLuhan returned with Corinne to Missouri in 1940 to finish his contract at St. Louis University and continue working toward his doctorate. Focus was a problem for him, but not because he had trouble concentrating or had more interesting things to do. To McLuhan, study and the pursuit of ideas were so fascinating that he had difficulty narrowing his dissertation investigation to a manageable topic. Everywhere he turned were ideas and theories that seemed to beg for his condemnation or his rapture. There were times in his life when McLuhan wondered if he was a dilettante, and this must surely have been one of those times.

McLuhan persisted, despite the problems of focus, and despite fatherhood, which he experienced for the first time in 1942 when son Eric was born. Although his own father had been a wonderful model of fatherhood to him, McLuhan was never really comfortable with the role for himself. Philip Marchand, one of McLuhan's most perceptive and thorough biographers, suggests, "It is almost certain that if McLuhan had not been

Catholic and if the pill had existed in 1942, Eric would have been an only child."

In any event, the presence of children in his life (and the couple were to have five more) did not deter McLuhan from his academic pursuits. In 1943 he finished his PhD from Cambridge, and the next year the McLuhans returned to Canada. They first went to Windsor, Ontario, where he taught at Assumption College. Two years later, he accepted a teaching post at St. Michael's College, University of Toronto.

Around this time, American literary magazines were accepting a small portion of McLuhan's writing. His recurring theme was the power of advertising, and his writings included specific warnings about the potential downfall of a society controlled by companies whose purpose was to make people want more of what they were selling. However, much of his work was far too complex in style and concept for mainstream audiences. For the first few years, his theories reached only other academics with similar ideas.

In 1951, Vanguard Press published McLuhan's first book of cultural criticism. *The Mechanical Bride* was a collection of essays on advertising and its effects on North American society. It had a difficult birth, taking over six years from manuscript to published page, and McLuhan showed a stubborn side in his dealings with his editors. He claimed they didn't understand his work. They claimed it was his style of writing that made it incomprehensible. *The Mechanical Bride* never became a bestseller, but it did receive positive reviews.

At the University of Toronto, McLuhan gradually began to formulate an idea that culminated in the 1964 publication of the book that turned him, almost overnight, into a guru of the counterculture, and which has since been translated into more than 20 languages. The phenomenal success of *Understanding Media* led to a host of invitations for McLuhan to address major corporations and brought into daily speech his often-quoted phrase: "The medium is the message."

Even though members of the hippie counterculture adopted McLuhan's phrases and terms, few people totally understood his ideas, not even his fellow intellectuals. The collection *Who Was Marshall McLuhan?* includes an anecdote from Arthur Porter, a colleague at the University of Toronto, who reported, after attending a party where they were both guests: "I returned home to tell my wife that I had met a most incredible chap. I have never met anyone quite like him. But I didn't know what the hell he was talking about most of the time."

Whether or not he was understood, McLuhan had the public's attention. He moved swiftly from speaking engagements to media appearances. In March 1967 he was featured in a segment of the

NBC series *Experiments in TV.* Other guest shots on
various networks followed. It was ironic that
McLuhan appeared on television, considering the
ideas put forward in *Understanding Media* were
based on his firm belief that television was the
bane of society. But in the 1960s, an age of new
and spontaneous enlightenment, the outrageous,
if largely incomprehensible, actions of a brilliant,
articulate and enigmatic 50-something man were
not criticized by his smitten followers.

That is not to say he was without critics. There
were people both in and out of academia who dis-
missed him as a charlatan and claimed he pur-
posely obfuscated his speeches and writings in
order to appear profound. Others said he had sold
out to fame. Some declared his ramblings absolute
nonsense. To make matters worse, in the late
1960s McLuhan received a one-year grant for
$100,000 to conduct research on media and com-
munications at New York's Fordham University.
His own salary from the grant was $40,000, far
more than his Toronto colleagues were earning.
The result was more criticism. McLuhan's reaction
to such criticism was a shrug.

McLuhan published several more books in the
1960s, mostly collaborations with others. He continued a hectic lecturing schedule, both at home at
the University of Toronto and as a guest lecturer in
other institutions. From 1963 until his death,
McLuhan was director of the Centre for Culture
and Technology at the University of Toronto, where

his Monday-night seminars became a who's who of intellectuals and celebrities. Among the luminaries who attended these public sessions were Prime Minister Pierre Elliott Trudeau; musicians Glenn Gould, John Lennon and Yoko Ono; Russian poet Yevgeny Yevtushenko; journalist Malcolm Muggeridge; and countless throngs of unnamed but thoroughly convinced students. In 1964 he was named a Companion of the Order of Canada, and between 1965 and 1969 he received five honorary doctorates from a list of universities that included the University of Windsor (1965) and his alma mater, the University of Manitoba (1967).

His personal drive and energy were not enough to stave off a medical catastrophe. In 1967, after suffering for years from excruciating headaches and blackouts, McLuhan was diagnosed with a tennis-ball–sized tumour at the base of his brain. Although it was not malignant, the tumour had to be removed or it would have continued to grow until it caused blindness or insanity. The delicate surgery took close to 17 hours. McLuhan's extraordinary sense of humour is illustrated in *Who Was Marshall McLuhan?* by an exchange that took place in his recovery room less than an hour after the surgery ended. When the surgeon asked the groggy McLuhan how he was feeling, he replied, "It depends on how you categorize feeling."

McLuhan's physical recovery was amazingly rapid, and for the first time in years he was free of the debilitating headaches. But he was never the same after the surgery. His phenomenal memory had been dampened, and he found he could not recall details of books he had read. He began to have difficulty remembering people's names, and he sometimes got lost in familiar places. Although only 56, he looked and acted like a much older person, irritable and quarrelsome over the slightest thing. His sense of humour remained, but he no longer had the stamina to work as hard as he had. His wife, Corinne, and several friends, including his younger brother, Maurice, came to the Centre to keep it running and to help McLuhan with his writing. More books were published: *Counterblast* in 1969; *From Cliché to Archetype* and *Culture is Our Business* in 1970. But more and more it seemed that McLuhan was a spent force. Newspapers and journals no longer bothered to review his books. The end of McLuhan's influence came with the publication in 1972 of *Take Today*, a convoluted treatise on everything he had ever espoused.

Honorary degrees and additional awards were still being conferred: an LLD from the University of Alberta in 1971 and DLitts from the universities of Western Ontario and Toronto in 1972 and 1977 respectively. He received the Institute of Public Relations (Great Britain) President's Award in 1970. In 1971 he was given the Christian Culture Award from Assumption University and the Italian President's Gold Medal in recognition of his work on mass media. In 1973 he was appointed a consultor of the Pontifical Commission for Social Communications at the Vatican.

More honours and speaking engagements followed, but the late 1970s were less active professionally for McLuhan. His six children were grown, and many of them were successes in their own right. He continued to come up with ideas for books, some of which managed to catch the eye of publishers, and he continued to teach and speak publicly, although at a gradually reduced pace. In 1977 he negotiated a three-year extension of his contract with the Centre at the University of Toronto. He was still eager to continue working.

Just two years later, on September 29, 1979, McLuhan suffered a severe stroke that robbed him of his ability to read, write or speak more than a few words. The man who had taught most of the Western world about the deep and wondrous possibilities of communication had lost his ability to communicate. On December 31, 1980, Marshall McLuhan died at home in his sleep. He was 69 years old.

McLuhan tried to tell us that one day technology would control us, not the other way around. It seems he foresaw the world of today, where people are unable to spend one hour without checking their BlackBerries; where traffic accidents occur because a driver's attention is taken away to answer a cell phone; where children on a cross-country road trip spend more time watching videos than scenery.

A large amount of Marshall McLuhan's work
remains unpublished, and much of what was published has drifted into obscurity. But his ideas
remain out there in acoustic and visual space.
They may well have more relevance today than
ever before.

CHAPTER EIGHT

Emily Murphy
(1868–1933)

Nothing ever happens by chance, everything is pushed from behind.

–Emily Murphy

IN THE MIDST OF AN ONTARIO BLIZZARD ON MARCH 14, 1868, Emily Ferguson came into the world, howling louder than the wind. The storm that welcomed her was a prelude to the storms of controversy this feisty little woman was to stir up during her memorable lifetime.

Emily's parents, Isaac and Emily Ferguson, third-generation Irish-Canadians, raised their six children to believe that both girls and boys were to share in the rewards as well as the work, although it was not as if the Ferguson children endured a harsh life. Isaac was a prosperous Cookstown, Ontario, businessman who was well able to afford household servants. But his children, four boys and two girls, had chores and responsibilities that they carried out with quiet, if sometimes reluctant, obedience.

They were good Christians, but the Fergusons condoned responsible social drinking and card playing, and the family enjoyed a lively and wholesome life together. As a child, Emily learned to sew, cook and entertain. Under the watchful eye of her brothers and the amused gaze of her parents, she and her sister also learned to ride, climb and play field sports.

At 15, Emily was sent off to Bishop Strachan School in Toronto, the prestigious all-girls boarding school. She was not a remarkable student, but she enjoyed the boarding school atmosphere and was conscientious in her studies. Although at first sad to be separated from her happy family life, Emily was not lonely for long. Her two elder brothers, attending the equally prestigious all-male Upper Canada College, came regularly to take her for walks or out to dinner. On one of these outings they were accompanied by a tall, handsome blond friend named Arthur Murphy.

Arthur joined them several more times and soon became the love of Emily's life. Shortly after his graduation, Arthur, who was 11 years her senior, became established as the new Anglican minister in nearby Forest, Ontario. They were married on August 24, 1887, at the Ferguson home in a large and elaborate wedding, surrounded by well-wishing friends and relatives of both Ferguson and Murphy families. Comfortably situated, and content with each other, Arthur and Emily soon had three little daughters to share their life: Kathleen (b.1888), Evelyn (b.1890) and Madeleine (b.1892).

Two sad events disrupted the young couple's life during this time. Emily's father, Isaac, was diagnosed with cancer and died in 1889. And in April 1893, Emily and Arthur's youngest daughter, Madeleine, then less than one year old, also died. After a period of mourning, the family gathered strength from one another and gradually resumed its happy life.

As a well-respected and effective minister, Arthur received requests to work with struggling congregations in the area, so over the next few years the family moved regularly. In September 1896, when Emily was 28, she gave birth to their last child, another daughter, whom they named Doris. The baby's older sisters, who were now eight and six, were eager to provide entertainment, and with domestic help from household servants, Emily had time on her hands. She became involved in community activities, assisting Arthur with his parish visits to the sick and lonely and, using the phenomenal memory she had developed in school, helping him select appropriate biblical passages for use in his sermons.

It was about this time that Arthur's bishop asked him to consider doing missionary work. The change meant almost constant travel from one Ontario mission to another, with stays of a few months in each place. It was a difficult adjustment for the family to make, but Emily and the girls pulled together and supported Arthur in his vocation, becoming involved in the mission work at each posting. The living conditions and human suffering Emily saw during these years left a lasting impression on her. She began to record her thoughts in diaries, detailing everyday events and her heartfelt reactions to them. With Arthur away for long hours at a time, and the children cared for by hired help, these daily jottings became the high-light of Emily's days. They later formed the basis for much of her published material.

In 1898 an opportunity arose to do missionary work in Liverpool, England. The Murphys decided to take it, and that summer the family sailed to Britain for a totally new adventure. With its lush countryside, fragrant estate gardens, great cathe-drals and famous theatres on the one hand, and its grime, vulgarity and abject poverty on the other, England was a study in contrasts for Emily. She wrote articles about what she saw and felt, using the pen name "Janey Canuck" in honour of her homeland.

Emily and Arthur enjoyed their year in Europe. They enrolled the girls at a boarding school, and Emily was able to travel with Arthur to Germany and Holland, where he accepted preaching engagements. The experiences filled Emily's mind and her diaries.

On their return to Canada at the end of 1899, the Murphys settled in High Park in Toronto. Once again Emily and Arthur were close to their families. Their two older daughters, Kathleen and Evelyn, boarded at Havergal College in Toronto, coming home on long weekends and holidays. For the next two years, Arthur preached and Emily compiled and edited the writings she had produced in Europe, eventually publishing her first book, *The Impressions of Janey Canuck Abroad,* in 1901. The book was a brief account of her experiences overseas, and it became popular in England and in Canada. On the strength of her prose and insights, Emily began writing regular articles for the *National Monthly of Canada,* a magazine owned by a member of the Murphys' social circle. Janey Canuck was becoming widely read and widely known.

Then in autumn 1902, tragedy struck. Doris, who was six and still at home, came down with diphtheria. Within days, she was dead. It struck the family very hard. Arthur, whom Emily had taken to calling "the Padre," had just the year before suffered a severe bout of typhoid fever. His health began to deteriorate. The remedy prescribed by his physician was a change of location, so the Murphys, grief-stricken but together, moved to Swan River, Manitoba, where Arthur tried his hand at managing a timber lot.

In Swan River, Emily continued to write for the *National Monthly,* and Arthur gradually built up his health and his timber business. The girls were enrolled in boarding school in Winnipeg, and Emily filled the void by writing book reviews for the *Winnipeg Tribune* and helping Arthur with bookkeeping for the timber lot. By 1907 it was time to move again.

Emily was 39 years old and Arthur 50 when they arrived in what would be their permanent home, Edmonton, Alberta. The Murphys loved Edmonton from the start. Kathleen and Evelyn, now poised young ladies of 19 and 17, welcomed the new life in an exciting and sophisticated city on the civilized edge of the great western frontier.

With her daughters involved in Edmonton's lively social life, and Arthur delving into the lucrative possibilities of the city's booming real estate industry, Emily's writing flourished. New York's Cassell and Company published *Janey Canuck in the West* in 1910 and *Open Trails* in 1912.

But writing was not Emily's only pastime. She had seen numerous examples of poverty during her time as a preacher's wife and had been further enlightened on the subject, particularly poverty's effects on women, through her charitable work with various women's groups. She became the leader in a campaign to have the Dower Act made into law. The act, passed in 1911 after years of lobbying, ensured a married woman's rights to share property held in common with her husband. Before that time, a man could sell property without his wife's consent, and a widow who had put equal work and effort into a farm could be left penniless unless her husband left the proceeds to her in his will.

This was not Emily's only success. She became the first female member of Edmonton's Hospital Board and helped establish the Edmonton chapter of the Victorian Order of Nurses. She was the Canadian secretary of the Society of Women Journalists and president of the Canadian Women's Press Club.

In 1916, after hearing that a group of prostitutes were being brought before a judge who might not be sympathetic to the backgrounds that contributed to their downfall, Emily and some female friends attempted to sit in on the court proceedings. They were asked to leave on the grounds that the testimonies were not fit to be spoken in mixed company. Emily and her colleagues agreed, and in a move that kept the press busy for days, they began lobbying the attorney general to have the case heard by a female judge. The attorney general not only concurred with the petition, but invited Emily to let her name stand for the position. Weeks later, at the age of 48, Emily Murphy was sworn in as the first woman magistrate in the British Empire.

Her Honour Justice Emily Murphy became a well-respected magistrate, using her phenomenal memory to quickly grasp the details of cases brought before her. It was later suggested that she had her own biases—against aboriginals and foreigners, for example—and she had only marginal patience with repeat offenders. But on the whole, she seemed to understand her role and did her utmost to carry out her duties in a fair and balanced manner. She also continued to write. *Seeds of Pine* was published in 1914 and *The Black Candle*, a riveting story of the evils of drug addiction, in 1922.

In 1928, Emily was recruited by friends and colleagues in the Canadian Women's Press Club to petition the Supreme Court of Canada for an interpretation of the term "person" in the British North America Act, Canada's constitution at the time. In what became known as the Persons Case, Emily and four other prominent women (Nellie McClung, Henrietta Edwards, Louise McKinney and Irene Parlby), dubbed the Famous Five, petitioned the Supreme Court and then the British Privy Council, and finally succeeded, on October 18, 1929, in having women declared "persons" under the law. (For a more complete account of the events leading up to the Persons Case, please see Chapter Six on Nellie McClung in this book.)

A personal outcome for Emily was a series of petitions put forward by women's groups to have her appointed to the Senate. She was considered, but the honour of becoming the first woman senator in Canada went to Cairine Wilson. Emily took the personal disappointment in characteristic stride. The success of the Persons Case had had widespread positive effects for women all over Canada, giving them the right to vote and hold public office, and Emily felt she had done what was required.

She continued her work as a judge and remained active in her many causes. She published two more books, to the delight of her reading public: *Little Canadian Cousins of the Great North-Western Provinces* in 1923 and *Bishop Bompas* in 1929.

Emily Murphy's happy and energetic fight to help the women of Canada achieve a better life ended on October 26, 1933. She died quietly at home in her sleep from a brain embolism, which was likely complicated by a long history of diabetes. She was 65.

CHAPTER NINE

Lester B. Pearson
(1897–1972)

Happiness in work is an essential ingredient for happiness in life.

–Lester B. Pearson

LESTER BOWLES PEARSON'S EARLY LIFE AS THE SON OF A Methodist minister did not prepare him socially for the diplomatic service, but it did form the strong character and tact for which he became known. Born in Newtonbrook, Ontario, on April 23, 1897, the middle of three sons of Edwin and Anne Pearson, he grew up in a loving home that stressed the principles of uprightness and patriotism, and the evils of liquor, gambling and tobacco.

The young Pearson boys moved with their parents to various small Ontario towns where their father served as parson. In 1913, young Lester, or "Mike" as he was known, entered Victoria Methodist College of the University of Toronto. Less than a year later, Great Britain declared war on Germany. An energetic recruitment campaign began in Canada in early 1915, and Pearson, about to write examinations to complete his second university year, enlisted and went to Macedonia as a private in the Medical Corps.

After almost two years of treating the wounded and dying, he was sent to Oxford University in England to train as an officer. Pearson, who had a long-standing interest in flying, began training with the Royal Flying Corps, but after only a few weeks he was struck by a bus in London as he waited on a curb in the spring of 1918. He was injured seriously enough to be sent home. Although disappointed at not being able to follow through on what he felt was his patriotic duty, Mike's job as a navigation instructor, which he took to finish off his service commitment, gave him a taste for teaching.

After the war ended, Pearson re-enrolled at the University of Toronto. He graduated in June 1919 and immediately took a job at a meatpacking firm in Chicago. He soon tired of the work and realized he was craving the intellectual stimulation that university had provided. His fond memories of England drew him back to Oxford, where he received a scholarship for graduate studies, an endeavour that resulted in a teaching job in 1923 at his old alma mater, the University of Toronto. With history as his specialty and athletics as his extracurricular pursuit, Pearson, at 26, enjoyed an interesting and varied life as a young university lecturer. It was during the early 1920s that he married one of his students, the young Maryon Moodie, a native of Winnipeg who was studying in Toronto.

Pearson's interest in history led him to begin writing a book on the United Empire Loyalists, which indirectly caused his career to take a sharp turn. In 1926, research on the book took him to the National Archives in Ottawa for the summer. While there, he met several influential politicians, among them O.D. Skelton, deputy minister of External Affairs, and J.S. Woodsworth, member of Parliament for the Independent Labour Party. Pearson must have impressed both men, for they kept in touch with him on his return to Toronto.

Two years later, Skelton recruited Pearson into the Department of External Affairs. At 31, Pearson left academic life and moved, with Maryon and baby son Geoffrey, to Ottawa to become a diplomat in Canada's fledgling foreign service. His first international placement was a summer posting to Washington, DC, in 1929. The following January he was sent to London, England, with a small delegation to attend the London Disarmament Conference, and in subsequent months he went to other countries on a number of short missions. He became accustomed to travelling, and his easygoing manner with people from all walks of life made him a natural choice to accompany government officials on overseas assignments.

In 1932, Pearson attended the League of Nations' World Disarmament Conference in Geneva and impressed his superiors to such an extent that he was given a choice posting the following year—first

secretary to Vincent Massey, High Commissioner to
Great Britain. By this time, the Pearsons had a second child, daughter Patricia, and the young family
travelled to London to take up residence in a lively
and affluent section of the city.

Much of Pearson's work as a junior diplomat
was clerical, but some unusual tasks were required
of him. One of these came about as the result of
Prime Minister Mackenzie King's love of antiqui-
ties. The World War I bombing of Westminster, the
British Parliament, had left the area in ruins. Today
at Kingsmere, King's estate in the Gatineau Hills,
visitors can admire a number of gigantic stone
slabs from Westminster thanks to Lester Pearson,
who organized their acquisition and transport back
to Canada.

As much as Pearson liked London, he was
pleased when, in 1942, he received a posting to
Washington, DC, as assistant to Leighton McCarthy,
Canada's representative in the United States.
Well known in Washington circles, McCarthy liked
his new assistant and gave him access to high-
ranking American government officials, who
quickly warmed to him. Pearson proved once
again that he was the right man for the job.
Speeches and press releases were his tasks, but
courteous informality and a quick sense of
humour became his trademarks. McCarthy died
in 1945, and Pearson, at 48, succeeded him as
Canadian ambassador to the United States. He
remained in that post for a year, at which time

he was named undersecretary of state for External Affairs and brought back to Ottawa.

Louis St. Laurent was minister of External Affairs, and Pearson spent two productive years as undersecretary in St. Laurent's department. The men got along well, and Pearson established an easy yet respectful rapport with his new superior. In summer 1948, when Mackenzie King retired and St. Laurent took over as leader of the Liberal Party of Canada, Pearson received his first ministerial appointment. To fulfil the requirement that ministers had to represent one of the two political parties, Pearson ran for and won the Liberal seat in the Ontario riding of Algoma East on October 25, 1948. At 51, Lester B. Pearson was a member of Parliament.

The Pearsons, like many other political couples, had to make some adjustments to their new life. Pearson's strict Methodist upbringing was at odds with Ottawa's high-flying social milieu, but he adapted well to its expectations. His teetotalism had, over the years in the diplomatic service, gradually given way to more liberal views on alcohol, and he maintained an active social schedule without falling prey to excesses.

Maryon was not as adaptable. Impressed by the sophisticated and well-bred people they were now in a position to know, Maryon was at the same time uncomfortable about how she would fit in. Her discomfort often led her to display a lack of civility with the public, the press and people in the Pearsons' social circle. A fan of late-night parties and risqué language, Maryon displayed a distinct lack of tact at dinner parties, where she often made unpleasant references to Pearson's shortcomings, making it plain to all present that she considered her husband a bumbling fool. He appeared to suffer her barbs with characteristic good humour, but Mike Pearson must have been hurt by their implications.

There was even a hint of scandal in the early 1950s when it was rumoured that Maryon was having an affair with Graham Towers, governor of the Bank of Canada and a married man. The rumours, whether rooted in fact or fiction, resulted in a cooling off of Pearson's friendship with Towers and did little to endear Maryon to the Ottawa elite. Some well-known public figures who travelled in the same social circles did little to hide their dislike of Maryon. American Secretary of State Dean Acheson made it no secret that he thought her rather bad mannered. Arnold Heeney, then Canadian ambassador to Washington, wrote in his diary: "She gives me the creeps and I cannot be at ease with her—because she dislikes me I suppose. She has managed, so unnecessarily, to acquire so many critics, poor woman." And in another, more unequivocal, diary entry he stated: "I can't stand Maryon Pearson."

The rancour arising from her behaviour likely added to the already tense situation at home. The Pearsons were going through the typical trials parents face when their children enter adulthood.

Daughter Patricia, at 21, moved to London, Ontario, to train as a nurse and, against her mother's wishes, to pursue a relationship with the man she later married. Son Geoffrey, in his second year at Oxford, went ahead with his marriage even after his father tried to persuade him to wait.

The strife at home did not seem to have a negative effect on Mike's political life. Smiling and affable, bow-tied Pearson made friends wherever he went, but it was not due only to down-home charm. In every country of the world in which he had dealings, Pearson was becoming known for his outstanding diplomacy and his ability to bring out the best in the people who worked with him.

As president of the General Assembly of the United Nations (UN), a post that he took in 1952, he was responsible for bringing harmony to several acrimonious debates. He also had a more serious, aggressive side. Pearson was convinced that peace among nations was possible, but he felt that many world leaders were dealing ineffectively with problems. He desperately tried to convince leaders that peace was more a matter of understanding other cultures than imposing Western values on the world. In a lecture at Princeton University in 1953, he suggested that "the most far-reaching problems arise not between nations within a single civilization, but between civilizations themselves."

In 1956, major world powers were on the verge of a third world war as a result of the Suez

Crisis. When the United States and Britain withdrew promised funds to build the Aswan High Dam, Egypt retaliated by blockading the Suez Canal. Britain, with assistance from France and Israel, invaded Egypt in an attempt to regain control of the crucial waterway. The UN was thrust into the fray, with Canada and the United States expressing serious opposition to the aggression. Despite ongoing lack of support from John Diefenbaker, who was Conservative foreign affairs critic at the time, Pearson, with characteristic diplomacy, managed to suppress the animosity and avoid what would surely have been a disaster of major proportions. His idea was to establish a UN police force in the region to lessen hostilities and to supervise a ceasefire, allowing Britain, France and Israel to withdraw without losing face.

On November 3, 1956, the United Nations Emergency Force, a precursor to the blue-bereted peacekeeping force, was created in a unanimous UN General Assembly vote. Less than a year later, in October 1957, Pearson was awarded the Nobel Prize for Peace for his efforts. He was the first Canadian ever to receive the honour.

A world crisis averted, Pearson turned his attention to political matters at home in Canada. In 1958 he became leader of the Liberal Party and leader of the opposition, as John Diefenbaker had led the Conservative Party to power in 1957. Pearson used the next few years to build up talent in the party and to put forward several progressive policies. He also developed a close relationship with John F. Kennedy, who became U.S. president in 1961. Neither man had much respect for John Diefenbaker. Support for the Diefenbaker government was beginning to crumble in Canada because of its poor decision making and its lack of diplomacy during the 1962 Cuban Missile Crisis. In the 1963 federal election, the Conservatives were defeated, and Pearson took his place as prime minister with a minority government.

During his time in office, Pearson had a hand in creating some of the most progressive legislation ever to be passed in Canada. He set up the Royal Commission on Bilingualism and Biculturalism, which led to a policy of providing government services in both French and English, and he established the Royal Commission on the Status of Women. In 1965 he signed the Canada-U.S. Automotive Products Agreement (Autopact), which created thousands of jobs in the Canadian automotive industry. He introduced the national code of labour, which established minimum wage and maximum work-hour guidelines. He introduced crop insurance for farmers and increased the old-age pension and veteran allowances. He set up the Canada Pension Plan, the Canada Assistance Plan (which covered unemployment insurance and social assistance) and Medicare.

Pearson was also responsible for the creation of Canada's red and white maple leaf flag in 1964–65. His cross-Canada contest for a design to replace the Red Ensign energized Canadian feelings of patriotism and set the stage for the exciting and memorable centennial celebrations in 1967, the same year Canada hosted the celebrated and successful Expo 67 in Montréal.

As proud Canadians tucked away their photos and memorabilia at the end of the centennial year, Pearson announced his retirement. Under his tutelage and waiting in the wings was Pierre Elliott Trudeau, who replaced him in December 1967.

Pearson continued to be active in political circles, teaching international relations at Ottawa's Carleton University and working with various committees on international development. On December 27, 1972, five years after retirement and after a two-year battle with cancer, Lester B. Pearson died at his home in Ottawa. He was 75.

Although he held the office of prime minister for less than four years, his reputation had already been established and his influence felt for the previous two decades. His diplomacy and his contributions earned him many distinctions over the years, including Companion of the Order of Canada and the Order of Merit from Queen Elizabeth II. Pierre Trudeau and Jean Marchand, who had both benefited from his wise and caring mentorship, carried on Pearson's legacy of statesmanship.

The man many believe was Canada's finest prime minister is buried in a small cemetery in La Pêche, Québec, formerly known as Wakefield, a quaint village on the Gatineau River. Pearson's final resting place is less than an hour's drive from Canada's Parliament Buildings and three hours' drive from the Lester B. Pearson International Airport in Toronto.

CHAPTER TEN

Louis Riel
(1844–1885)

I have devoted my life to my country. If it is necessary for the happiness of my country that I should now cease to live, I leave it to the providence of my God.

–Louis Riel

LOUIS RIEL WAS BORN ON OCTOBER 22, 1844, IN A HOME IN the Red River Settlement of Rupert's Land (now Manitoba), which he eventually shared with eight younger brothers and sisters. Life at the Riel home was happy, lively and productive. Riel's father, Louis Sr., owned and operated the community's flour mill, its giant millstones powered by the nearby Seine and Red rivers. Although not wealthy, the Riels were respected members of the community, descended from hearty and respectable forebears.

Louis Riel's mother, Julie (nee Lagimodière), was the daughter of a fur trader who had been granted a generous strip of fertile land along the Red River in exchange for services rendered to Lord Selkirk, governor of Rupert's Land. Riel's father was Métis, one of the thousands of people of mixed French and aboriginal blood who spoke

French and adhered to the Catholic faith. As descendants of the *coureurs de bois*, they upheld the legacy of their forefathers and were industrious and sociable people, ideally suited to the rigours of the settler's life.

From the outset, Louis Riel Sr. was a positive role model for his young son. Not well educated in any formal sense, the senior Riel nevertheless had a solid understanding of the role the Métis were playing in the settling of the West, a role that included providing a substantial supply of furs to the Hudson's Bay Company (HBC) and generous assistance to the Scottish settlers who were unaccustomed to the harsh prairie conditions. He was also a leader among his people.

In the mid 1840s the HBC attempted to gain a monopoly over the fur trade and bolster its profits by gradually lowering prices paid to Métis trappers. The trappers responded by selling their pelts to Americans traders, who paid higher prices. The HBC was potentially facing enormous losses. Rather than trying to match prices paid by the Americans, the HBC slapped restrictions on the Métis trappers, requiring that they agree not to sell their furs to anyone else, with a penalty of imprisonment for breaking the agreement. A group of courageous Métis, led by Riel Sr., spent several months petitioning, marching and conducting small but effective protests. They finally won, and free commerce was again a reality for the Métis trappers.

This was the environment in which young Louis Riel was raised. He soon understood that justice was not necessarily on the side of the just, but that careful planning and collective strength could win out. As a good son, young Louis followed his father's example, and as a good student, he was able to take it even further.

At the age of 13, Louis went to Montréal to study at the Seminary of St. Sulpice and, subsequently, at the Collége de Montréal. Already fluent in French, English and Cree, young Louis adapted well to the rigid discipline and rigorous curriculum, which included studies in classical Greek and Latin as well as philosophy and elocution.

In 1865 he became a law student in the office of Rodolphe Laflamme, leader of the Rouge Party, a marginal group of Montréal intellectuals who were embroiled in a bitter struggle against Confederation, which they saw as an extension of British colonialism. Laflamme, a lawyer and later Québec cabinet minister, made a huge impression on the young Métis, but so did other influential people Riel met while studying law, including Wilfrid Laurier (future prime minister of Canada), Louis-Joseph Papineau and George-Étienne Cartier.

During those years, young Riel also saw how leaders could wield power to turn one person against another. Citizens of Canada East (later Québec) who sided with the British in their support of Confederation earned titles, land and position, while those who resisted became pariahs. Riel saw a parallel in the Métis situation in the northwest.

When the Dominion of Canada was established in 1867, Québec was part of the new country, but the British North America Act gave Québecers significant jurisdiction over matters of language and religion. Riel was again in a position to see the power of the collective voice.

Riel left Québec shortly after Confederation, but he did not return directly to the Red River Settlement. There were as yet no roads through the Canadian Shield, so travellers were invariably forced to trek south into the northern American states. Riel likely stayed at several different locations in Michigan or Minnesota and spent time teaching in order to earn enough at each stop for the next leg of his voyage.

He finally arrived in his birthplace in 1869. His father had passed away five years earlier, but he found his widowed mother, and his five siblings who remained at home, in good health and well looked after by extended family and a caring community. The Red River Settlement was now concentrated around the small but thriving town of Winnipeg, and the area's population had exploded to nearly 10,000. There was still an active fur trade thanks to the groundwork done by Riel's father, and residents appeared to have adequate access to the necessities of life. But conditions were about to deteriorate.

The Hudson's Bay Company was negotiating with Ottawa to transfer its holdings in Rupert's Land to the new Dominion. There was some urgency because of the fear that the United States would annex the area. Prime Minister Sir John A. Macdonald named William McDougall, an Ontario bureaucrat, to be lieutenant-governor of the new territory. McDougall, a pompous and unlikeable man with a history of ill-treating aboriginal people on Ontario's Manitoulin Island when he was commissioner of Crown lands, was a dubious choice, possibly selected specifically for his shortcomings. Riel had likely heard of McDougall's appointment, and his reputation, while he was still in Montréal.

As December 1, 1869, the date set for the transfer of the territory, approached, residents of the Red River became increasingly uneasy. They were aware that by joining Canada they were in danger of being sidelined in an administration made up mostly of English-speaking Protestants. Moreover, plans were to accept the territory into Confederation, not as an equal partner with the rest of Canada, but as a colony with diminished rights. By the time McDougall and his small party of surveyors and bureaucrats reached the Red River Settlement, the Métis were ready for them. An unarmed group led by Riel and several other respected Métis met them and refused to allow them to enter the settlement. McDougall and his party retreated in anger.

Over the next few days, the Métis met and dis-
cussed their options. They formed the National
Committee of the Métis, which sent a letter to
McDougall, telling him that they would not accept
him as their leader since they had not been con-
sulted about his appointment. The letter was
signed by the group's president, John Bruce, and
Louis Riel, secretary. To further indicate the seri-
ousness of their intentions, the Métis set up a
roadblock at St. Norbert, Manitoba, a village
between the Red River Settlement and Pembina,
North Dakota, the small U.S. border town where
McDougall had gone to wait out the resistance,
which he anticipated would soon die down. He
clearly did not realize the depth of Métis resolve.

On November 2, 1869, Riel and his followers,
again unarmed, took possession of the HBC head-
quarters at Upper Fort Garry. When McDougall
learned of this action, he stole into the Red River
Settlement and on December 1, the day scheduled
for the territorial transfer, he read a proclamation
that effectively took authority for the territory out
of the hands of the Hudson's Bay Company. However, because McDougall hadn't established any
effective replacement for HBC authority over the
settlement, a vacuum was created in the territory's
governance. The Métis quickly set up a provisional
government, with Louis Riel as its president, to fill
the void.

Riel was not naïve. He knew the government
in Ottawa was not going to accept the Métis

takeover of the territory it had hoped to colonize with Europeans. He also knew that a significant portion (almost one-third) of the residents of the territory were English-speaking Protestants who favoured joining Canada, even though it would mean less-than-equal status with the existing provinces. He set about attempting to gain support from, or at least start a dialogue with, the English-speaking residents.

On January 29, 1870, Riel, and his fellow residents drew up a set of conditions under which they would consider joining Canada. This included demands that Ottawa pay for its title to the territory, that Métis and aboriginal claims to the land be conceded, that land be set aside for their children and for the Roman Catholic Church and that the local government be elected.

While the provisional government was discussing the terms it would negotiate with Ottawa, a small band of anti-French, anti-Catholic Orangemen, who called themselves Canada Firsters, arrived in the Red River Settlement. They were outraged that a group they looked upon as insolent, illiterate half-breeds should challenge the decisions of Her Majesty's loyal servants in Ottawa. The Firsters combed the countryside for recruits to take up arms against the Métis. In one of their sweeps, they came across a young Métis, who attempted to run when they approached. Young Norbert Parisien, a mentally handicapped teenager, was no more a spy than he was a king.

He ran out of fear. Nevertheless, the Firsters decided to use the boy to set an example to other Métis. After capturing him and leaving him overnight in an unheated church during the frigid Manitoba winter, they threatened to hang him. Nearly frozen from his overnight ordeal and now faced with death, young Parisien grabbed a pistol and tried to get away, shooting and mortally wounding one of his captors who came after him on horseback.

The group recaptured Parisien and brutalized him for hours. He died from a blow to the head that a Firster named Thomas Scott bragged of delivering. Scott, a staunch Orangeman recently arrived from Northern Ireland, was a violent racist who had been in trouble with the law since his arrival on this side of the Atlantic. Riel and his men soon captured Scott, along with his fellow Firsters, and imprisoned them at Upper Fort Garry. Duly tried and convicted of the murder of Norbert Parisien, Thomas Scott was executed by a firing squad organized by Louis Riel's provisional government on March 4, 1870. Reaction to the execution was not immediate, but it was significant.

Less than a month after Scott's execution, delegates from Red River and Ottawa settled on the terms presented by Riel's provisional government. These terms received parliamentary approval and became law in the Manitoba Act on May 12, 1870. Language, property and religious rights were guaranteed for the Métis nation, and the people of

Manitoba entered Confederation as equal citizens of Canada.

But Riel did not fare as well as the province he had fought for. At the end of the summer of 1870, a reward was offered for his capture for his leading role in the execution of Thomas Scott—an act the government of Canada proclaimed to be sedition. Riel went into hiding.

Trouble continued to brew. Ottawa ignored land claims that had been guaranteed under the Manitoba Act, and the Métis people decided they needed Riel's leadership once more. In October 1873, they elected him member of Parliament for Taché. Receiving conditional amnesty from Prime Minister Macdonald, Riel decided to travel east to take his place in the House of Commons. Anticipating that he would be apprehended the moment he made an appearance in the House, he went into hiding near Plattsburg, New York.

Over the next two years he was elected twice more to represent his people in Ottawa, but he was never able to take his seat in the House. His name on the roll had its effects, however. As historian J.M. Bumsted observes: "Riel now saw his candidacy as a national matter, throwing down the gauntlet to Ontario Orangemen on behalf of French-Canadian Catholicism everywhere in the Dominion. The strategy was clearly designed to identify the cause of the Métis in Manitoba with French Canada. Riel also now understood that he need not try to take up his seat for this strategy to be effective."

Realizing the man's power even in absentia, the government expelled Riel from the House and in February 1875 banished him from Canada for five years. Riel remained in the United States for the next year, suffering what some believe was a mental breakdown. There are differing accounts of his condition at this time. On two previous occasions (1870 and 1871), Riel had suffered similar attacks of high fever, swollen joints and delirium. The previous bouts were diagnosed as encephalitis (brain fever), which developed after untreated infection from pneumonia. The bout in 1876 was more serious and was perhaps worsened by the depression he surely suffered from being separated from his family and friends. He was smuggled out of the United States by friends in Québec and brought to a mental hospital in Montréal, where he was declared insane. During the two years he remained in the asylum, he occasionally ranted that he was not insane but had been sent by God to free his people.

In the late 1800s, insanity was often diagnosed after one incident of violence or upset was observed in a patient. Some patients who exhibited no symptoms at all were declared insane simply because there was insanity in their families. A further indication of the thin logic that often went into such a diagnosis was the generally accepted belief that insanity was related to tuberculosis. Statistics of the time showed that the proportion of people with tuberculosis in insane asylums was double the proportion in the general population. As a result, it was erroneously assumed that people with tuberculosis were more likely to be insane than those who did not have the disease. As Riel had developed pneumonia more than once, it is possible he fell into that spurious statistical category. In any event, the claim that Riel was insane should not be taken as infallible.

After his release from hospital in 1878, he returned to the United States, where he met and became engaged to Marguerite Monette (also recorded as Monet) Bellehumeur, a beautiful young Métisse who was living in Montana. They were married on April 28, 1881. Riel was 36; his bride 20. He remained in the United States, taking a teaching post at St. Peter's Mission in Montana. On May 4, 1882, the Riels' first child, son Jean, was born. Their daughter, Marie-Angélique, followed on September 17, 1883. Around this time, Riel toyed with the idea of giving up his Canadian citizenship and adopting the United States as his homeland. But the people of the Canadian West still needed him.

The Canadian Pacific Railway was being built to transfer thousands of European settlers, mostly from England and Scotland, to the prairies with promises that they would have their choice of land. The Métis were once more to be pushed into the background. At the same time, there was a scurvy epidemic and widespread starvation as a result of repeated crop failures, particularly in aboriginal settlements. And there was growing animosity to the North-West Mounted Police (NWMP), the police force commissioned by Ottawa to keep the aboriginals and Metis in check.

Riel returned to Canada with Marguerite and the children. They settled for some time in St. Vital, then moved on to the large Métis settlement at Batoche (in present-day Saskatchewan). Once again, Louis Riel was to become a leader of his people.

On March 25, 1885, an incident at Duck Lake, northwest of Batoche, escalated tensions. A group of disgruntled and starving Métis and aboriginals led by Gabriel Dumont stormed the government-run Duck Lake settlement and raided the food stores. In the battle that followed, several men from both sides were killed. It was the beginning of two months of aggression. Riel, in an attempt to show support for his compatriots, set up a stockade at Batoche and imprisoned several government officers captured at Duck Lake. Meanwhile, Ottawa dispatched militia units, whose ranks were swollen with untrained, undisciplined civilians recruited from their office jobs and farmlands to fight in the service of the government of Canada against the man who had been labelled a traitor to the new Dominion.

Riel faced the advancing troops with courage and a belief in the righteousness of the Métis cause. His diary entry of April 21, 1885, illustrates his feelings: "I have seen the giant—he is coming. It is Goliath...they will know the Almighty is preparing to inflict retribution upon them."

In early May 1885, troops began a series of assaults on Batoche. On May 12 the small village was captured, and Riel was once more on the run. On May 15, having decided that too many lives were at risk, Riel surrendered to General Middleton, who promised an amnesty for the Métis people. On July 6 a formal charge of treason was laid against Riel, and two weeks later his historic trial began in Regina. The trial was a travesty, with a less-than-stellar defence based, despite Riel's wishes to the contrary, on a plea of insanity and on inaccurate and misleading translations of witness statements. Riel was found guilty on August 1 and sentenced to execution. Ottawa ignored a recommendation for mercy, and subsequent appeals were denied. A number of Riel's well-placed friends from Québec and Manitoba tried to intervene, and crowds swarmed government offices in Québec in his support. It was all to no avail.

Shortly after 8 AM on November 16, 1885, after receiving the last rites, 41-year-old Louis Riel was hanged before a small group of NWMP officers, a coroner and Riel's priest. He was buried in the cemetery of St. Boniface Cathedral, 15 kilometres from the small cabin on the Red River where he was born.

The cabin is still there. It has been designated a National Historic Site, operated jointly by Parks Canada and la Société historique de Saint Boniface, and is open during the summer months for interpretive tours in French and English. There are no longer clothes hanging to dry in the prairie breeze. The garden is nothing more than a patch of weeds that stubbornly fight their way through the lawn between strategically placed park benches. But there is a spirit there. It is seen on the sober faces of eager schoolchildren who come to show their respect to this man who was once hunted as a rebel, who was hanged as a traitor, and who is now remembered as the Father of Manitoba.*

---

* For the complete story of Louis Riel, see the book *Louis Riel*, by Dan Asfar and Tim Chodan, published by Folklore Publishing.

CHAPTER ELEVEN

David Suzuki
(1936–)

Education has failed in a very serious way to convey the most important lesson science can teach: skepticism.

–David Suzuki

IF YOU HAVE HEARD OF A FISH THAT RUNS FASTER THAN IT swims, or if you have been concerned about the destruction of tropical rain forests, it is likely that you can trace your introduction to the topic to Dr. David Suzuki. Suzuki, one of the most widely recognized scientists in the world today, has spent the last 40 years bringing science to people of all ages and educational levels.

Born in Vancouver, BC, on March 24, 1936, to second-generation Canadian parents of Japanese descent, David Takayoshi Suzuki began his early life in an apartment attached to the family's dry-cleaning business in the Marpole district of Vancouver. In 1942, after Japan entered World War II on the side of the Axis Powers, the family was interned along with other Japanese Canadians in Slocan, BC. It was a difficult time for David, his twin sister, Marcia, two younger sisters, Aiko and

Dawn, and their parents because they were forced to live with thousands of other people in cramped quarters with no indoor plumbing. David was also alienated from most other children in the camp because he did not speak Japanese. Although they were proud of their Japanese heritage, the family spoke English at home. Instead of playing with the other children, David spent many pleasant hours with his father, Kaoru, fishing and exploring the pristine forests and lakes that bordered the camp. It gave young David a chance to learn about and appreciate nature.

After four years in Slocan, the Suzukis started over, this time in Ontario. They spent one year near Windsor and then moved to Leamington, where David and his father resumed their weekend fishing and hiking trips. At the age of nine, David already had a respectful relationship with nature, which was nurtured by his father. Kaoru Suzuki also began encouraging his only son to excel at public speaking—a skill that no doubt bolstered David's confidence and later ensured his success as a media personality.

In 1953 the family moved again, this time to London, Ontario, where David's father joined his brothers in their business, Suzuki Brothers Construction. From Grade 10 until he graduated, David attended London Central Collegiate Institute, where he not only excelled at academics and public speaking, but was also elected student council president in his senior year. According to his biographer Ron Wideman, Suzuki's campaign speech was understated but effective: "I'm not a football player. I'm not a basketball player. I'm not part of the in-group. But I have good ideas, and you should vote for me." And they did.

David's work on student council did not interfere with his studies. His fine academic record earned him a scholarship to study science at Amherst College in Massachusetts, where he graduated, cum laude, with a degree in biology in 1958 at the age of 22. He then enrolled at the University of Chicago to continue his studies at the graduate level. His intensive study of genetics and research with fruit flies earned him a PhD in zoology in 1961. Newly titled Dr. Suzuki, along with wife Joane (his high school sweetheart) and their new baby daughter Tamiko, moved to Tennessee, where David took a research position in the biology division of the National Laboratory in Oak Ridge.

David was happy in his job. He found the research exciting and the climate welcoming. What he found impossible to accept was the racism he witnessed. The era of the early '60s was a time of strained race relations between blacks and whites, particularly in the southern United States, where blacks were treated as second-class citizens. Denied their basic human rights, many young blacks began peaceful protests against the conditions. Suzuki, with acute memories of his own family's experiences in Slocan, joined the National

Association for the Advancement of Colored People. As its first non-black member, he did his best to publicly denounce the treatment his fellow members were receiving.

In 1962, discouraged by the apparent lack of progress in the civil rights movement, Suzuki returned with his family to Canada's more diverse and accepting social climate. He took a teaching job at the University of Alberta in Edmonton, but after enduring the frigid temperatures for one winter, the family, now numbering four with the addition of son Troy, moved back to David's birthplace. In Vancouver, he joined the faculty of the University of British Columbia to teach and continue his research on fruit flies.

David's exposure to the civil rights movement in Tennessee led him to join the Japanese Canadian Association and the Canadian Civil Liberties Association on his return to Canada. He maintained an active membership in both organizations, but the bulk of his time was spent on his research. His long days and nights in the laboratory eventually paid off for science, but his personal life suffered. In 1965, shortly after the birth of the Suzukis' third child, Laura, Joane and David separated. They were divorced two years later.

Although it was a year of personal misfortune, 1967 proved to be professionally successful for David. He managed to breed a chemically mutated fruit fly that was unable to withstand temperatures

higher than 29°C. This had implications for biolog-
ical pest control: rather than killing insect pests
with chemicals, scientists would be able to breed
insects that died naturally at high temperatures,
passing on their heat-sensitive genes to other
insects in the wild before they died. It was a ground-
breaking discovery that caught the attention of the
National Research Council and the National Cancer
Institute, both of which immediately increased
project funding for his research. The discovery
propelled Suzuki to instant fame in the scientific
community, and in 1968 he was chosen as the
Canadian delegate to the International Congress on
Genetics in Tokyo.

Additional research grants enabled Suzuki to
increase his staff at the University of British
Columbia. By the early 1970s he had nearly two
dozen researchers and technicians working on his
team. Two years after his fruit-fly discovery, he
was approached by CBC Television to host four
half-hour shows on science topics. Suzuki was
already familiar with the power of television.
While in Edmonton, he had been a guest on a
campus science program that aired on a community channel. During that time he had become
aware of television's potential for informing the
public about scientific ideas. The series out of Vancouver was short-lived but successful, and by 1971
he was hosting his own series, *Suzuki on Science*.

At 35, Dr. David Suzuki was fast becoming a
local celebrity. It wasn't long before his name had

cross-country recognition, and over the next few years he received invitations from around the world to study, teach and present papers. His reputation took him to France, Puerto Rico, Russia, Germany and various points in the United States.

The success of *Suzuki on Science* led to the offer of another show, *Science Magazine*, which ran out of Toronto. Conscious of the abrupt turn he was taking in his career, Suzuki was nevertheless aware of the need for public education on science matters. He had become increasingly concerned about the negative possibilities of genetics research and the potential for harm to the environment. In 1974 he took a leave of absence from his work at the University of British Columbia and moved to Toronto, hoping to use the media to make people more aware of the need to examine ethical and social aspects of science. His knowledge, poise, charm and youth, coupled with the public speaking skill he had acquired under his father's diligent coaching, came together beautifully. In no time at all, David Suzuki was a media personality.

The CBC radio show *Quirks and Quarks* followed *Science Magazine* and was, in turn, followed in 1979 by a new television series, *The Nature of Things with David Suzuki*, a weekly one-hour show that drew viewers like a magnet. It was informative, but more importantly, it was entertaining and accessible to a broad audience. By 1984 the series was seen in more than a dozen countries around the world and reported an average of 1.8 million viewers per episode.

Suzuki's subsequent projects concentrated on environmental issues and pollution. The 1985 series *A Planet for the Taking* encouraged viewers to think and act more responsibly toward the environment. *Amazonia*, a program that first aired in 1989, delved into the depletion of the world's rain forests. Suzuki's influence was not limited to television. He also became an award-winning author of articles in scientific and mainstream journals and newspapers. He has written more than 35 books on a variety of science-based topics. His autobiography, *Metamorphosis: Stages in a Life*, published in 1987, is dedicated, not surprisingly, to his father.

His awards date back to 1972, when he was named Outstanding Japanese-Canadian of the Year. He received the Canadian Human Rights Foundation Award in 1975, and in 1976 was named an Officer of the Order of Canada. This honour was followed by the 1985 Governor General's Award for Conservation and the 1986 UNESCO Kalinga Award for his research. He claimed the Canadian Booksellers' Association Author of the Year Award in 1990, garnered several ACTRA and Gemini awards for his television work, and has received honorary doctorates from 15 universities around the world.

Much of Suzuki's recent work has been in Canada's First Nations communities. He believes

Native elders hold a vital key to the survival of our planet. His relationships with First Nations people have earned him five Native names and adoption by two tribes.

In 1990, Suzuki and his second wife, Dr. Tara Cullis, a fellow scientist, established the David Suzuki Foundation, a non-profit organization dedicated to the search for innovative ways to support sustainable ecology. They have passed on their love of the planet and their commitment to our role in its protection to their two daughters, Severn and Sarika. In 1992, Severn, then age 12, accompanied Suzuki to the Earth Summit Conference in Rio de Janeiro, where she addressed the delegates with an impressive degree of her father's poise and dedication.

Suzuki and Cullis currently live in Vancouver, where they manage the Foundation's activities. Suzuki retired from his teaching post at the University of British Columbia in 2001 and enjoys spending time with his family. He continues to accept occasional guest lectureships and television spots in his ongoing mission to teach younger generations to be more sensitive to the vital role we all play in the survival of our planet.

CHAPTER TWELVE

Pierre Elliott Trudeau
(1919–2000)

Reason before passion.

–Pierre Elliott Trudeau

STATESMAN, JOKER, SOPHISTICATE, WORLD TRAVELLER, DEVOTED father—Joseph Philippe Pierre Yves Elliott Trudeau was arguably one of the most dynamic, intelligent, controversial and engaging prime ministers Canada has ever had. You could love him or hate him, but as many journalists and public figures discovered, you could not ignore him. From the trademark red rose in his lapel to his rapier-sharp one-liners, which often caught even the jaded press by surprise, Trudeau was an unconventional politician.

Raised in the bosom of an affluent, bilingual Montréal family, Pierre had many advantages as he was growing up. His father, Jean-Charles Emile Trudeau, was a Montréal lawyer who became a millionaire while still in his 30s when he sold his chain of service stations to Imperial Oil. When he died in 1935, at the age of 47, he was a millionaire several times over. Pierre, his older brother Charles, his younger sister Suzette and their mother Grace continued to enjoy the privileged lifestyle the elder Trudeau had established for them. Along with travel, sports and other cosmopolitan pursuits, young Pierre immersed himself in the disciplined atmosphere and the liberal education offered by Montréal's Collège Jean-de-Brébeuf, where he developed a lifelong love of art and literature.

He followed his father's path into law, graduating with honours from the Université de Montréal in 1943 at 24 years of age. After practicing law for several months in Montréal, Trudeau was accepted at Harvard University, earning his MA in political economy in 1945. The following year he entered the École libre des sciences politiques in Paris, then enrolled at the London School of Economics.

In 1948, perhaps having seen enough of the world from the inside of a classroom, Trudeau began a walking tour of Europe, the Middle East and Asia. His facility with languages and his magnetic personality gave him many unique experiences on his odyssey, which took him to Bulgaria, Greece, Turkey, Poland, Austria, Hungary, Germany, Yugoslavia, Palestine, Burma, India, Hong Kong, Cambodia, Thailand and China. Many of these countries were either in the throes of revolution or just recovering. When Trudeau returned to Canada in 1949, his democratic yet idealistic philosophy was beginning to take shape.

Shortly after his return, Trudeau was involved in the first of many encounters with what he felt were repressive social conditions. In Asbestos, Québec, a mining town in the Eastern Townships, a battle had erupted between the provincial government, headed by Maurice Duplessis, and an increasingly militant labour force. Duplessis was intent on keeping the unions in line, while the unions were fighting for improved working conditions and pay. Trudeau, who was critical of the Duplessis government's policies and supportive of the workers' cause, became involved with the strikers, using his knowledge of the law to give them free advice.

Although his speeches were more proselytizing than practical, they brought Trudeau to the attention of police. Anyone associated with the strike was treated with suspicion. Trudeau and a friend were arrested and held when they were on their way to a gathering, although they were never charged. Ultimately, the strike action was successful. The miners negotiated a settlement and returned to work. For Trudeau, it was a good training ground for his future career in politics.

In September 1949 he accepted a post as junior economist in the Privy Council. The move to Ottawa put him in touch with the country's power brokers, and, accustomed as he was to travelling in upper-middle-class circles, he quickly became part of the elite. For the next several years, Trudeau spent his time at his work, at his various athletic pursuits and at his writing. He wrote personal memoirs as well as political criticism. He also took time to travel once more.

Between 1951 and 1955, when he was in his early-to-mid 30s, Trudeau took an extended foreign tour, this time to Africa, Europe and Asia. He even managed to thumb his nose at Canadian sensibilities about communism by visiting Russia and the Crimea, recording his experiences in a series of articles published in Montréal's *Le Devoir* newspaper.

On his return to Montréal, Trudeau's pursuits became somewhat more actively political. In the autumn of 1960, Trudeau accompanied his long-time friend, publisher Jacques Hébert, and several left-wing Canadian activists on a three-week tour of the People's Republic of China. It was another trip that Trudeau recorded for posterity, with a diary co-written by Hébert, later published as *Deux innocents en Chine rouge* (*Two Innocents in Red China*).

As Kevin Christiano points out in his 1994 biography: "Travel to Trudeau meant solitude without loneliness, selfhood without self-absorption." Travel allowed him to dream about what nation building in Canada could look like. He continued to teach and write, developing a reputation as a brilliant intellectual and an unrepentant loner, given to escaping alone or with one companion on canoe trips into his beloved Canadian wilderness. But his escapes into the hinterland were about to become rare. On November 8, 1965, Trudeau won the federal Liberal seat in the Mount Royal riding of Montréal and was off to Ottawa to serve his constituents.

The following two years were, in many ways, monumental for Trudeau. Prime Minister Lester B. Pearson named him parliamentary secretary. Then in spring 1967, Trudeau became attorney general and a vocal and active minister of Justice, proving himself to be a pragmatic reformer, introducing changes to several laws pertaining to divorce and sexual behaviour of consenting adults. His widely quoted statement "The state has no place in the bedrooms of the nation" succinctly summed up his philosophy toward legislation of personal matters.

Over Christmas 1967, Trudeau travelled to Tahiti, partly for relaxation, but more significantly, for Canada, to decide whether to run for the leadership of the national Liberal Party. His decision to run was greeted by near-hysteria from a public bored with straight and stodgy Canadian politicians. Pierre Elliott Trudeau was a star—a shy but sophisticated, charismatic playboy, known for occasional antics that gave print-hungry journalists countless front-page photo-ops. In no time at all, it seemed, Canada, particularly Canada's youth, was gripped by what the press called Trudeaumania. The term, allegedly coined by NDP MP Tommy Douglas, was an apt description of the wave of interest in politics that swept the nation.

Young, miniskirted teenyboppers, peaceniks in peasant dresses, long-haired dropouts and back-to-the-land hippies, many of whom had never before shown an interest in party politics, joined the brush-cut, white-collared, suit-and-tie crowd to support him. Trudeau was a different breed of politician—a sandal-wearing fellow who could quote Schopenhauer and Timothy Leary with equal accuracy; who had lived in foreign countries but always chose to return to his beloved Canada; who had grown up in the lap of luxury yet who spent wisely and ate organically. Pierre Elliott Trudeau was the New Canada.

On April 16, 1968, delegates to the Liberal Party of Canada convention in Ottawa declared Trudeau their leader. Within the month, Lester B. Pearson resigned as prime minister, and Trudeau took over the role. On June 25 the same year, Trudeau and his fellow Liberals managed an impressive landslide victory in the federal election, winning close to 60 percent of the seats.

Trudeau's time in office was enormously successful. He led Canada through some of the country's most turbulent yet ultimately most defining years. Between 1968 and 1971, the Official Languages Act was adopted, Québec struggled through the FLQ crisis and citizens from one coast to the other were showing an unprecedented pride in being Canadian.

Trudeau continued to surprise the country. In March 1971, he announced his marriage to a 22-year-old flower child. He had met Margaret Sinclair in 1967 while on vacation in Tahiti. By 1971, Margaret had moved to Ottawa from her home in Vancouver to work for the Department of Manpower and Immigration, and a quiet courtship began. They were married on March 4, 1971, and the following Christmas Day their first son, Justin, was born.

Margaret was 29 years younger than Pierre, immature and ethereal. At first the differences in their ages and lifestyles were seen as fascinating— a romantic real-life fairy tale occurring on our own doorstep. But the fairy tale quickly gave way to the realities of political life. The birth of two more sons, Alexandre (Sacha) in 1973 and Michel in 1975, thrust Margaret and the family into the spotlight. Trudeau's image changed from carefree playboy to devoted and energetic father, and he was frequently photographed romping with one or more of his beautiful sons. Margaret, feeling abandoned in the vast spaces of 22 Sussex Drive, began to exhibit irrational behaviour, which terminated in a mental breakdown severe enough to land her in hospital for almost two weeks in 1975. Although Margaret eventually recovered, their marriage never really did.

In 1976 the separatist Parti Québecois was elected in Québec. At a time when Trudeau needed, perhaps more than ever before, the support of family, he and Margaret separated. While leading the country through what many felt was its most critical period, he continued to be actively involved in the lives of his three boys, and he refused to air his personal problems in the media. Margaret, meanwhile, romped with the Rolling Stones in a Toronto hotel suite and flitted off to New York to become an actress. The couple never reunited.

In May 1979, the Liberals were defeated in a general election by the Progressive Conservatives led by Joe Clark, and Trudeau resigned as prime minister on June 4. In November he announced that he would resign as leader of the Liberal Party, but less than a month later, Joe Clark lost a vote of confidence in Parliament, and his government fell. Neither his personal troubles nor the difficulties of leadership were enough to dissuade Trudeau from fighting for the Canada he believed in. A few days later, he said he would lead the Liberals into the next election.

In February 1980, the Liberals were re-elected, and Trudeau was once more prime minister. Over the next four years, he led the Liberals and Canadians through the potentially divisive Québec referendum of May 1980 and the 1982 repatriation of the Canadian Constitution.

In February 1984, Trudeau went for a walk in an Ottawa snowstorm to contemplate his future. He emerged on February 29 to announce that he was stepping down as Liberal leader. He was named a Companion of the Order of Canada the following year in recognition of his contribution to Canada. Trudeau had left politics, but he continued to make his unflinching Canadian federalist ideals known through his incisive writing.

Pierre and Margaret Trudeau were brought back together for a brief sharing of public grief in November 1998 when their youngest son, Michel, aged 23, was killed in an avalanche in the Rockies.

On Thursday September 28, 2000, the world reacted with heartfelt sympathy when Trudeau's remaining sons made the following press announcement: "Justin and Sacha Trudeau deeply regret to inform you that their father, the Right Honourable Pierre Elliott Trudeau, passed away shortly after 3:00 PM."

Pierre Elliott Trudeau's death from cancer just weeks before his 81st birthday took one of the world's great statesmen and one of Canada's finest visionaries.

Notes on Sources

Margaret Atwood

Atwood, Margaret. *Negotiating With the Dead: A Writer on Writing.* New York: Cambridge University Press, 2002.

Davey, Frank. *Margaret Atwood: A Feminist Poetics.* Vancouver: Talonbooks, 1984.

Mallinson, Jean. *Margaret Atwood and Her Works.* Toronto: ECW Press, 1991.

Rosenberg, Jerome H. *Margaret Atwood.* Boston: Twayne Publishers, 1984.

Sandler, Linda. "Interview with Margaret Atwood." *The Malahat Review,* 41 (January 1977).

Tommy Douglas

Margoshes, Dave. *Tommy Douglas: Building the New Society.* Montréal: XYZ Publishing, 1999.

McLeod, Thomas H., and Ian McLeod. *Tommy Douglas: The Road to Jerusalem.* Edmonton: Hurtig Publishers, 1987.

"T.C. (Tommy) Douglas." *Weyburn Review* website. http://www.weyburnreview.com/tommydouglas.

"Tommy Douglas voted Greatest Canadian." CBC website. http://www.canada.com/news/national.

Terry Fox

Scrivener, Leslie. *Terry Fox: His Story.* Toronto: McClelland & Stewart, 1981.

Zola, Meguido. *Terry Fox.* Toronto: Grolier, 1984.

Wayne Gretzky

Leder, Jane Mersky. *Wayne Gretzky.* Mankato, MI: Crestwood House, 1985.

Wayne Gretzky official website. http://www.upperdeck.com/athletes/waynegretzky.

Wilker, Josh. *Wayne Gretzky.* Philadelphia: Chelsea House Publishers, 1998.

Sir John A. Macdonald

Berton, Pierre. *The National Dream: The Great Railway.* Toronto: McClelland & Stewart, 1975.

Lamb, W. Kaye. *History of the Canadian Pacific Railway.* New York: Macmillan, 1977.

Waite, Peter B. *John A. Macdonald*. Markham, ON: Fitzhenry & Whiteside, 1999.

Wilson, Keith. *John A. Macdonald and Confederation*. Agincourt, ON: The Book Society of Canada, 1983.

Nellie McClung

BC Archives website. http://www.bcarchives.gov.bc.ca. "Nellie McClung 1873–1951."

Benham, Mary L. *Nellie McClung*. Markham, ON: Fitzhenry & Whiteside, 2000.

Burton, Sarah. "The Person Behind the Persons Case." *The Beaver*, October/November 2004, 14–19.

Centre for Canadian Studies at Mount Allison University website. http://www.mta.ca/faculty/arts/canadian_studies/ (follow the links to "Famous Women in Canada" one of the "About Canada Study Guide Multimedia Resources").

Monaghan, Anne. *The Story of Nellie McClung*. London ON: London Council for Adult Education, 1986.

Marshall McLuhan

Gordon, Terrence. "Marshall McLuhan." Marshall McLuhan web site. http://www.marshallmcluhan.com/gordon.html.

Marchand, Philip. *Marshall McLuhan: The Medium and the Messenger*. Toronto: Random House, 1989.

Marchand, Philip. "Marshall McLuhan." Marshall McLuhan website. http://www.marshallmcluhan.com/marchand.html.

Marshall McLuhan official website. http://www.marshallmcluhan.com.

Nevitt, Barrington, and Maurice McLuhan. *Who Was Marshall McLuhan?* Toronto: Stoddart, 1995.

Emily Murphy

Mander, Christine. *Emily Murphy: Rebel*. Toronto: Simon & Pierre, 1985.

Sanders, Byrne Hope. *Canadian Portraits: Famous Women*. Toronto: Clarke, Irwin, 1958.

Lester B. Pearson

Bothwell, Robert. *Pearson: His Life and World*. Toronto: McGraw-Hill Ryerson, 1978.

English, John. *The Worldly Years: The Life of Lester Pearson*. Toronto: Alfred A. Knopf, 1992.

Heeney, A.D.P. *The Things That Are Caesar's: The Memoirs of a Canadian Public Servant*. Toronto: University of Toronto Press, 1972.

"Lester B. Pearson." Biography on the CBC "Greatest Canadians" website. http://www.cbc.ca/greatest/top_ten/nominee/pearson-lester.html.

Louis Riel

Bumsted, J.M. *Louis Riel vs Canada: The Making of a Rebel.* Winnipeg: Great Plains, 2001.

Charlebois, Peter. *The Life of Louis Riel.* Toronto: NC Press, 1975.

"Louis Riel." University of Saskatchewan Library website. http://library.usask.ca/northwest/background/riel.htm.

MacEwan, Grant. *Between the Red and the Rockies.* Toronto: University of Toronto Press, 1952.

Ricketts, Bruce. "Louis Riel—Martyr, Hero or Traitor?" Mysteries of Canada website. http://www.mysteriesofcanada.com/Canada/riel.htm.

David Suzuki

Beggs, Mike. "David Suzuki: Gladiatorial Geneticist." Canada's Digital Collections website. http://collections.ic.gc.ca/heirloom_series/volume6/224-225.htm.

"Dr. David Suzuki." Biography on the Order of British Columbia website. http://www.protocol.gov.bc.ca/protocol/prgs/obc/1995/1995_DSuzuki.htm.

"Dr. David Suzuki." Saxton Speakers Bureau website. http://www.saxton.com.au.

Webb, Michael. *David Suzuki: Superstar of Science.* Toronto: Copp Clark Pitman, 1991.

Wideman, Ron. *David Suzuki.* Markham, ON: Fitzhenry & Whiteside, 1988.

Pierre Elliott Trudeau

Christiano, Kevin. *Pierre Trudeau: Reason Before Passion.* Toronto: ECW Press, 1994.

Our Last Farewell: Pierre Elliott Trudeau 1919–2000. Toronto: McClelland & Stewart, 2000.

Angela Murphy

Angela Murphy is a full-time writer with an extensive and varied background in education. She held positions as a university lecturer, public school administrator and curriculum consultant before deciding to pursue a career in writing.

A published author, Murphy has four children's books and several magazine articles currently in print. She is a freelance literary reviewer for the *Winnipeg Free Press* and the *Ottawa Citizen*. Her reviews have also been published in *Books in Canada* and *The Gazette* from Montréal. She is a member of the Writers' Union of Canada and the Manitoba Writers' Guild. Her previous book, *Canadian Crimes & Capers: A Rogue's Gallery of Notorious Escapades*, was one of the first books in the Great Canadian Stories series.

FOLK LORE PUBLISHING

MORE GREAT CANADIAN STORIES

CANADIAN CRIMES AND CAPERS: A ROGUE'S GALLERY OF NOTORIOUS ESCAPADES
by Angela Murphy
This book chronicles exciting and little-known accounts of murder and mayhem from across the country, revealing the dark underbelly of Canadian society.
$9.95 CDN • ISBN 1-894864-30-1 • 5.25" x 8.25" • 144 pages

CANADIAN WAR HEROES: TEN PROFILES IN COURAGE
by Giancarlo La Giorgia
From the battles of the great warrior Tecumseh to the escapades of flying ace Billy Bishop to the heroism of Princess Patricia's Canadian Light Infantry in Afghanistan, this book traces the Canadian experience of war through the centuries.
$9.95 CDN • ISBN 1-894864-35-2 • 5.25" x 8.25" • 144 pages

FAMOUS CANADIAN ACTORS: THE STORIES BEHIND TODAY'S POPULAR HOLLYWOOD CELEBRITIES
by Stone Wallace
Roll out the red carpet for the long list of actors and actresses from north of the 49th parallel who have lit up the marquee in Tinseltown. Read about the early lives of Pamela Anderson, Dan Aykroyd and Jim Carrey; learn how Mike Myers and Keanu Reeves got started in their careers and a whole lot more.
$9.95 CDN • ISBN 1-894864-43-3 • 5.25" x 8.25" • 144 pages

PIONEER CANADIAN ACTORS: THE STORIES OF EARLY HOLLYWOOD CELEBRITIES
by Stone Wallace
This book celebrates the Canadian men and women who showed the world that some of the most impressive acting talent comes from Canada. Learn about the careers of Donald Sutherland, Lorne Greene, Fay Wray, Christopher Plummer, Mary Pickford, William Shatner and more.
$9.95 CDN • ISBN 1-894864-42-5 • 5.25" x 8.25" • 144 pages

CANADIAN WOMEN ADVENTURERS: STORIES OF DARING & COURAGE
by Tamela Georgi & Lisa Wojna
This entertaining and informative book chronicles the fascinating exploits of strong Canadian women who influenced the course of Canada's history. Read about mountaineer Sharon Wood, astronaut Roberta Bondar, artist Emily Carr, poet E. Pauline Johnson, journalist Faith Fenton, nurse Jeanne Mance and many others who have pioneered new horizons for women.
$9.95 CDN • ISBN 1-894864-39-5 • 5.25" x 8.25" • 144 pages

Look for books in the *Great Canadian Stories* series at your local bookseller and newsstand or contact the distributor, Lone Pine Publishing, directly. In Canada, call 1-800-661-9017.